P9-DUK-654

STUDIES
IN
FRANKNESS

Of him, whose shape this Picture hath design'd.
Vertue and learning, represent the Mind W. S.

CONTENTS

INTRODUCTION

WHEN Adam and Eve were chased from a blameless Paradise, they were forced to cover that which it had never been a dishonour to reveal. It was not until the devil murmured in the branches that a knee became more guilty than an eyebrow, and the prophets of concealment would be wise to remember that the reticence which they account the chief of virtues was the first penalty paid by guilty man to an enraged deity. Thus, in expiation of the primæval disobedience, we are still cursed or blessed with a shamefaced diffidence; we are compelled to the public denial of many truths which we acknowledge in secret; from our cradles to our graves we hide behind a mask of prudent discretion, or mincing chicanery; and we still share with the Puritan the punishment imposed upon the world by Eve's complacency. The Puritan, in truth, forgetting the cause of his modesty, makes righteousness of necessity, and believes that in prolonging a garment or blinking an eye he is doing a reputable service to the cause of virtue. But he is only bowing his neck beneath the inevitable yoke ; he is only bearing his part in the universal condemnation.

Though reticence was our first and heaviest punishment, it did not come upon us without compensations. The mere command that man should clothe his nakedness was sufficient to create the love of adornment and its attendant vanity. So the manifold arts of dandyism and coquetry came into being ; and man, by giving a separate colour to his life, distinguished himself from the beasts who know neither ornament nor shame. Then, also, was born sin ; then lawlessness, which hitherto had recognised vice as little as virtue, became law, and parcelled out all the possible actions of mankind into right and wrong, involving the pristine simplicity in unnumbered complications. Modesty was invented to keep pace with restraint ; licence dogged the footsteps of obedience ; and the presence of death gave man his first lesson in the value of life. And with sin was born humour, which could not breathe in a perfect Paradise—humour which sweetens misery with a laugh, and sets our heaviest misfortunes in a just relation. But, that the new-made sinners might not too loudly exult, prudery was appointed the watch-dog of humour, and it is from the tangled combat of these opposites that wit and adventure, joyousness and romance, come forth victorious.

Life, then, whether we will or no, preserves its privacies and restraints, which have grown stronger by tradition, and whose imperious sway no lover of curiosity will resent. Thus, there are ordained for us a thousand intricate rules, in obedience to which we play the game or fight the battle of existence. Nor are they irksome, these infringements upon our liberty, since life is made interesting by prohibition, and since it is to them that we owe our morals, our manners, the very elegancies of human conduct. To dream or licence with equanimity is impossible. The most ardent worshipper of the red-cap would find no pleasure if once he realised his vain scheme of freedom, and happily the force of tradition is still strong enough to thwart his worst intention. But the Puritan has applied the laws of life, and others ten times sterner, to the art of literature, so that words are detected in flagrant criminality, and poetry has become a liveried convict.

The confusion of literature with its material possesses, like many another vice, the dignity of age. Yet its inveteracy is no palliation, and never had the vice less excuse than to-day, when the last subtlety of the art should be understood. Life, in its many-coloured relations, and in all its restless vicissitudes, is the proper field of literature. But while life is governed by the laws of habit and the empire, literature bows only to its own dictates. Knowing this single restraint, it is otherwise untrammelled as freedom itself; and he who would throw a needless chain upon it might as well attempt to stem the torrent or fetter the whirlwind. But the hopelessness of an enterprise seldom deters the foolish, and from the very beginning of time literature, poor innocent literature, has suffered a twofold misunderstanding. In the first place, its motive has been tried by the inexorable law of life; its every incident has been scrutinised by the cross-eye of moral censure; and each reckless Aristarchus has asked not how the parts perfect the whole, not how the episodes combine to a proper climax, but whether such adventures as decorate the narrative might enter into his own experience without a protest. In the second place, the creator has been pilloried for the sins of his own creatures. "Who drives fat oxen must himself be fat," and he who draws the character of a tall man must himself overtop six feet. The manifold and contradictory virtues and vices which give life and variety to a book are visited for punishment upon one devoted head. Heedless of logic or common sense, forgetting that a work of art —the result of a personality—is still impersonal, the censorious are wont to endow the inventor with all the attributes of all his characters. Thus Fielding in one aspect is as brave a spark as Tom Jones himself, in another blameless as the fair Sophia; and you shudder at the folly which would make Balzac one with the heroic world of passion and intrigue, of love and terror, of spendthrift extravagance and hard economy, which he has called into being.

But the end of impertinence is not yet reached. The Methodist who is convinced that nothing has a right to exist which does not exercise a beneficial influence upon conduct, has framed the converse axiom that none save a good man may write a good book. And more than this: the man should be good with the Methodist's own particular goodness. He must be prepared to wave aloft the flame-coloured banner of the conventicle, and his life will bear instant testimony to his genius. So the Methodist averting his eyes from poem or romance, turns criticism into a kind of indiscreet biography. The printed page need say nothing to him; he is content to rake in the dust-heap of the past; and should he discover the compromising evidence of one sin, he proceeds to a judgment, proud in the conviction that he is not only displaying his own intelligence, but is conferring a distinguished favour upon morality.

Naught else remains than to frame definitions, to fit the craft of letters with fantastic titles, or to condemn it for ever as an Exponent of the Ethical Life. The ethics, uncovered by this method of criticism, are as simple as the field is narrow; but the zealot consoles himself by making scandal a check upon his judgment, and by proving the dramas of Shakespeare masterpieces because the writer was a "kind man." The pursuit, indeed, has a charm for all such as love statistics, but even the statistician may feel a pang of regret when an accidental document compels him to revise a lifelong opinion of Shelley's art or morals. And how shall he esteem a work to which tradition has attached no name? To him, alas! the *Satiricon* must be a perpetual puzzle, since no ingenuity can disclose the *dossier* of its unknown author. But this perversity of judgment, which involves literature in inextricable confusion, is not permitted to interrupt the pursuit of humbler trades. Not even the wildest enthusiast would condemn a boot because it was cut from the hide of a vicious animal, or because the shoemaker devoted his leisure to whisky and sedition.

However, when once the censor has laid a heavy hand upon literature, he is not induced by reason to relinquish his grasp. But his pertinacity is never aroused to understanding. If only he could analyse his displeasure, he might discover that it is genius not impropriety that repels him. His reprobation proceeds less from morality than from lack of imagination. Incapable of disengaging life from its presentation, he forms an instant picture of the written word, which he straightway charges with the infamy of his own distorted vision. And first with an energy of condemnation he would exclude from the privilege of type all such words and phrases as are not heard at his own fireside. Nor could he pronounce a less apposite judgment; since between the written language and the spoken there is a complete divorce. It is by an accident that speech and literature employ the same symbols, and a formal expression instantly changes the value of the common currency. To conversation and oratory are appointed their own rules, while literature retains a special freedom. The tongue, in brief, is an enemy to literary expression, and Cicero showed himself keenly sensitive to his art, when, having composed the denunciation of Catiline in his study, he refrained from its delivery. Thus it is that the word for word report has killed the possibility of lasting eloquence. Time was when the orator translated his speech from the language of the voice to the language of ink and paper, before the eye of man might look upon it; to produce in silence the effect of sound and gesture, another phrase, another style are necessary; but the trick of shorthand has baffled his art, and henceforth there will be speaking in unrestrained volubility, but no persuasive oratory that will live in the closet.

So a thousand dishevelled words, which the primæval ban forbids us to use in familiar intercourse, may be proper matter for literature. These libertines of speech have a value which does not depend upon the ideas which they connote. They are, so to say, strong notes of colour upon the printed page, and their use is controlled not by morals but by taste. Yet it is not given to every scribbler to open the door to an indiscriminate rabble. Frankness is the privilege of genius alone. Where tone and style permit, and where courage comes to the aid of invention, there are few things that may not be said with dignity and distinction. But writers there are, to whom no freedom is permitted, in whose books a single word, innocuous elsewhere, gives you a shudder of disgust. Rabelais, on the other hand, is sovereign of himself. With a heartwhole laugh of wisdom he purged the last grossness of offence. Since he knew all things, and with a perfect humour set them in their proper places, no door was closed to his intrusion, no corner secluded from his prying eye. He might thrust his rake into the worst rubbish-heap and withdraw it unspotted from the contact. Nor are you surprised that he spent his life in reflective taciturnity, and was known to his contemporaries for a dreamer.

But the Puritan is not content with sentencing to outlawry these words, for which his starveling soul has no employ. A grumble is still heard when he has replaced outspokenness by a clumsy artifice of ceremonious delicacy. He would also sit in judgment upon the visions which literature evokes, upon the fanciful characters she portrays. He finds the poet wandering in a paradise of license, and straightway he would drive him out, bidding him cover his beautiful images with the clout of shamefacedness. This intolerance has never fallen short of its opportunity, and the Puritan, whose censure is but the expression of a private dislike, pretends that he is fighting the cause of the people. But genius does not "address its pen or style unto the people whom books do not redress," and, in warning the illiterate against such works as they are doomed to misunderstand, the Puritan does but stimulate an unrighteous pruriency. For the illiterate have no concern with such masterpieces, as might uncover to their eyes the hidden places of the earth. Content to feed their fancy on the vulgar novel, they should run no risk from the contamination of genius. Yet it is this anxiety for the people which, ever since Plato, has been the worst enemy of literature.

As the savage round the camp fire sings his song of bravery that he may feed the warlike spirit of his tribe, so Plato saw in poetry naught but a means of fashioning good citizens. Strange it is to find the acute philosopher ranged on the side of the "poor Indian." But Plato's business was with politics rather than with literature, and (for the moment) he would rather have banished all poetry from the perfect city of his imagination than have endangered the morals of a single leather-seller. Moreover, the poetry of Greece, though the highest form of art, was still intimately related to the worship of the gods, and, save in the poet's own esteem, it did not yet exist as an end unto itself. But this is less a question of art than of history, and presently Aristotle came to the aid of literature, declaring that pleasure was its aim, and that no poet need refrain from the presentation in words of such things as in life are painful or abhorrent.

Literature, then, is unconcerned with the improvement of the citizen, or the welfare of the state. A thing of beauty, it knows no law save the law of its own embellishment. It sings in the ear, it laughs in the brain. It has the touch of Midas and transmutes, with happier effect, whatever is common into gold. The ugly in life instantly changes to loveliness at its potent wizardry. The pain and misery of Philoctetes are informed with a noble majesty when once they have passed into the verse of Sophocles. "The Dean," said Stella, "could write finely about a broomstick," and thus, unconsciously maybe, put the case of artistic freedom in an epigram. To the artist, indeed, nothing comes amiss if only his treatment justify his choice. The unnoticed corners of reality, the distant provinces of devilry and magic—he is free of them all. His world, which embraces yet transcends the narrow world of life, knows not the limits which are set upon the hardiest traveller. And if he will he may envelop his puppets in an unknown atmosphere. He may lift them to a table-land where all things have a different meaning, where the literal is dead, where flagrancy is humour, where only the inartistic is ugly. Or he may imagine a country where the ten commandments do not run, he may deftly transpose vice and virtue, and he may do it with so invincible a joyousness that his fantasy is pure of offence. But into this gay kingdom the censor with his prying eye may never penetrate; for he will detect in its flowers the iridescence of a stagnant pool, and carry away a legend of horrors that he has never seen. He will turn the fairy tale of Petronius into a shameful reality, and cavil at the shadow-land of Poe because he finds it a patent outrage upon nature. He will recoil from whatever is frank and outspoken because his own withered tongue can only frame the catchwords of the newspaper, because his discoloured eye perverts merriment and sincerity into evilness of speech and thought. But his persecution, dangerous though it be, dies with his death, and is remembered only in the contemptuous indignation of his victim.

So romance, poetry, satire, have fought the double

battle with the difficulties of their art, and with those enemies who would limit the field of their enterprise. Nor have their enemies been constant in severity save at one point. Now they will condemn the supernatural as the enemy of faith, now they will pronounce the legends of brigandage a direct incentive to crime, but never will they swerve one inch from their denunciation of "passion" in whatever terms it be expressed. For them, at least, the unknown is not magnificent, and in a fury of hatred they resent a reference to the sentiment which can never be theirs. With as clear a reason might they cry out upon a heroine with blue eyes or red hair because a dark-eyed beauty is nearer to their heart. But they have always fought in defiance of reason, and while they have changed their weapons they have displayed a fierce persistence in the combat. Aristophanes, who tuned his lyre to satire, melody, or wit, and who hid the patriot behind a mask of laughter, was fiercely attacked in his own lifetime, and still appeared coarse and obscene to no less a critic than Plutarch.

But it was Catullus, hapless lover and impeccable poet, who first found the perfect answer to his assailants. With an energy of rage he destroyed Aurelius and Furius who dared to assume his character from his works, and who, judging his verses *molliculos*, would denounce the writer as *parum pudicum*. His triumphant answer has been echoed by a hundred poets at bay. "Nam castum esse," he wrote, with superb dignity,

"Nam castum esse decet pium poetam
ipsum, versiculos nihil necesse est."

And neither Ovid nor Martial* could wish a better defence, while our own Herrick would have placed at his book's end a translation which long since became classic: "Jocund his muse was, but his life was chaste." Thus should the cavillers be silenced, though the chastity of a poet's life does but little concern them. Thus might they learn to avoid a universal stumbling block were they not beyond guidance. Nor were the poets alone in the public displeasure. Romance fell early under the curse; the Milesian stories, those masterpieces of gaiety, which, destroyed by popularity, have floated down to us on the stream of memory and imitation, were esteemed disgraceful even by the Parthians; and there is no more entertaining criticism in ancient literature than the anecdote of Surena's hypocrisy, as related by Plutarch. It is thus the story is told in North's version:† "Surena having called the Senate of

* "Vita verecunda est, musa jocosa mihi": thus Ovid, and Martial does but give the same sentiment another turn: "Lasciva est nobis pagina, vita proba." Pascal, who is not a tainted witness, finds another, and a more liberal comment for the poet of the Epigrams: "L'homme aime la malignité," he writes: "mais ce n'est pas contre les borgnes, ni contre les malheureux, mais contre les heureux superbes; on se trompe autrement. Car la concupiscence est la source de tous nos mouvements, et l'humanité." An unexpected judgment, truly, and a strange conjunction.

† The Life of Crassus.

Seleucia together layed before them Aristides book of ribaldrie, intituled *The Milesians*, which was no fable, for they were found in a Romanes fardell or trusse, called Rustius. This gave Surena great cause to scorne and despise the behaviour of the Romanes, which was so far out of order, that even in the warres they could not refraine from doing evill, and from the reading of such vile books." There is a touch of comedy in the barbarian's lofty indignation against the levity of his enemies, who beguiled a tedious campaign with the best of light-hearted literature. But still more amusing is Plutarch's comment. "I will not deny," he writes with a cunning respectability, "but Rustius deserved blame: but yet withall, I say, that the Parthians were shamelesse to reprove these bookes of the vanities of the Milesians, considering that many of their kinges, and of the royal blood of the Arsacides, were borne of the Ionian and Milesian curtisans." Was there ever such a jumble of hypocrisies? The Romans were infamous to relieve the serious pursuit of war with a jest-book. So far Surena and Plutarch agree. But Surena, says Plutarch, was debarred from objection by the pedigree of his kings, which he at least could not control, and which might have turned the royal house to grave reflection. Here is no word in defence of Aristides and his fables; no scorn of the Parthian's folly; only a jumbled reprobation of accuser and accused. Nor was the censure of Rustius universal. For those there were who believed that Surena had himself put *The*

Milesians at the sack's mouth, thus repeating the trick played upon the innocence of Benjamin. And Surena's imposture is easily credible, since many a worse artifice has been contrived in the name of an acrimonious morality.

Thus at all times austerity has resented the pastime of the sage. Was not Heliodorus, whose worthy intention should have atoned for more than his innocent freedom, chased from his bishopric? Had Chaucer's splendid sincerity any better chance of escape than Boccaccio's delicate devices? Has not Shakespeare been judged as coarse as the Classics? Yet none ever so conclusively proved that "to the pure all things are impure" as Jeremy Collier. This notorious nonjuror, indeed, resumed in his single talent the prejudice of all the ages. He undertook a crusade against the theatre, and he possessed every qualification which the task demanded. He was stupid, ignorant, and energetic. Like the clown at a country fair, he belaboured all the talents with a bladder tied to a string, and so long as his blows were sounding he cared not for their effect. Gifted, moreover, with the trick of advertisement, he made himself a far greater place in the world than his merit warranted. He was, in fact, a pestilent fellow that every one knew, and the pillory aiding, he won a large share of that notoriety which appears to some more gratifying and which oftentimes is no less lasting than legitimate fame.

His moral arrogance was prodigious; never had a

corrupt universe known so splendid a castigation; and the esteem of his contemporaries fell but little short of his own pride. Congreve paid him the extravagant compliment of a reply, and Dryden (from indolence, let us hope) was driven to submission. Yet beyond an occasional vigour of phrase and an immense peevishness the man possessed no quality of taste or intelligence. So deeply was he absorbed in fault-finding, where no fault was, that reason and justice were out of his reach. A casual familiarity with the Classics merely led him still further astray, and he is prepared to applaud the blaspheming of Euripides, for instance, because that poet directed his assault against paganism, and never struck a blow at the orthodoxy of a non-juror! "When Pegasus is jaded," he wrote at the beginning of his tract, "and would stand still, he is apt like other Tits to run into every puddle." And truly Jeremy Collier's own was a jaded Tit, for she is never out of the mire.

Armed with a false definition, he easily demolishes the whole fabric of modern literature. "The business of plays," says he, "is to recommend virtue and discountenance vice;" and whenever he finds the drama of his age falling short of this ideal, he is transported with rage. Wit and humour, gaiety of invention, the necessity of amusement—these are nothing to him. He will confuse the playhouse with the pulpit, and attack all the poets with equal folly and brutality. They are obscene, says he; they are blasphemous; therefore away with them all from

Shakespeare to Tom D'Urfey. Hamlet's author, indeed, comes off badly from the trial. "He is too guilty," writes the censorious Collier, "to make an evidence; but I think he gains not much by his misbehaviour." Assuredly he profits not at all from the pulpit's point of view. And again: "Phedra keeps her modesty even after she had lost her wits. Had Shakespeare secured this Point for his young Virgin Ophelia, the play had been better contrived." Did ever lack of humour drive a man into greater folly? Ophelia spotless! Why not Hamlet sane? But Collier is unable to distinguish between his own world and the stage, that kingdom of paste-board and plank, where language assumes a separate meaning, and where the sea coast of Bohemia is authentic as London Bridge. So having laid it down most properly that to swear before women is not only a breach of good behaviour but a most unchristian practice, he is ready to abolish all plays, within the limits of whose five acts a single oath is heard. "A well-bred man," he declares with evident truth, "will no more swear than fight in the Company of Ladies," and if he were logical, he would perforce have condemned the alarums and excursions of Shakespeare as so many outrages upon good manners.

But it is blasphemy which tempts him to his highest flights. "Sometimes," he exclaims in the very climax of his denunciation, "sometimes they don't stop short at blasphemy." The offence is scarce credible, and the instances which this nonjuror is able to quote are warranted to send a thrill of horror through the most hardened atheist. Think of the naked levity of Lady Froth, who calls Jehu a hackney coachman ! And the monstrous profanation of the author who dared to give his Sir Sampson Legend the name of that hero who triumphed over the Philistines ! In spite of the *p* a covert attack upon the Christian faith is evident, and one shudders to think what had become of England without the timely intervention of Jeremy Collier. But the worst is not yet told. Vainlove, in *The Old Bachelour*, asks Belmour if he could be content to go to heaven. To Vainlove only one answer was possible. But did he give it ? Oh, dear no ! With the shameful flippancy of the stage he replied: "Hum, not immediately in my conscience, not heartily." And nowhere does Collier prove his moderation more nobly than in his comment upon this monstrous wickedness. Here indeed was an opportunity for pious wrath, but with a perfect reserve he stays the tide of reproach. "This is playing, I take it, with edged tools." These are his very words, and yet one would have thought that the impious Belmour had forfeited all his fingers !

Such is the man who presumed to detect the seven deadly sins and seventy-seven others in the works of Congreve ! He might as easily have sought crime in a lace-frilled shirt or a satin coat. The cold, intellectual presentation of life which we get in the incomparable *Way of the World* possesses wit, alertness, repartee, all the graces of spirited converse, but it possesses nothing else. The world, whose way Congreve pictures, is a world which Jeremy Collier never could have penetrated. For its gates are shut against the dullard and the pedant. Its inhabitants are not controlled by the laws which run outside the chartered domain. It is, in truth, an Abbaye de Thélème where the sole restriction is "what you will;" and no man can understand its merriment who does not first put off the superstitions of an interested piety. The actions, performed within its borders, are judged neither by their motive nor their result, but rather by the method and style of their performance.

In brief, the Artificial Comedy has no contact with actuality. You may pass it by in dislike if you will, but you may not set it in the dock prepared for the criminal's reception. Charles Lamb, the most inventive critic of our stage, pierced the mystery with a flash, and his luminous paradox is no paradox at all. Given the proper atmosphere, and Joseph Surface is a hero, if only he bear himself with a magnificent levity. As for Jeremy Collier, he made no attack upon Congreve, because he understood not one line of that master's composition. He thought he knew one language; his victim wrote another. And the fact that Congreve deemed it a gentleman's duty to reply to such a tangle of impertinence is a sad comment upon the England that was governed by William of Orange. But the insult to Congreve was not Collier's last offence. So hopeless was the confusion of this befogged Puritan, that he condemned Juvenal for all the sins lashed in his satire. "He writes more like a pimp than a poet," said he with accustomed elegance. . . . . "Such nauseous stuff is almost enough to debauch the alphabet, and make the language scandalous." Why did he not go one step further, and saddle the intrepid Jeremy with all the vices of obscenity and profanation which he ascribed without thought or reason to his betters?

But Jeremy Collier not only enjoyed the admiration of his age; he is still regarded as a literary Hercules who cleansed the dramatic stable of its filth. And never since have zealots been lacking to carry on his work of obfuscation and stupidity. The appearance of a masterpiece is sufficient to render the bloodhounds restless in their leash. No sooner was *Madame Bovary* printed in the pages of a review than imperial France shuddered for her virtue. The author was thrust with his publisher in the dock, and the arguments paraded against them are but an iteration of Jeremy Collier's fallacies. "Gentlemen," said the prosecuting counsel, doubtless with a majestic wave of his honest hand, "Gentlemen, did Madame Bovary love her husband, or did she even try to love him?" Thus the game of cross-questions and crooked answers was played, as it will be played another thousand times; thus literature was clipped again to the petty standard of the hour. On either side the discussion was inapposite. The attack pronounced the book a glorification of adultery; the defence, unyielding in folly, discovered in its pages a treatise upon education. And Flaubert—where was he in this genial interchange of absurdities? He had written a great book: wherefore he was disgraced, and his escape from justice was a miraculous accident.

Baudelaire fared worse; he was tried, and he was condemned. Accused of all the crimes suggested by his poetry, he would have been for ever silenced had the rage of the crowd prevailed against him. But never once, to use his own phrase, did he "confuse ink with virtue;" never once did he accept the foolish verdict of the rabble. When the trial was finished a friend asked him if he had expected acquittal. "Acquitté!" he replied; "j'attendais qu'on me ferait reparation d'honneur." Yet he knew no reparation, save the esteem of poets, and the ultimate restoration of his criminal works. Nevertheless he recoiled not from the popular verdict. He saw clearly the bedevilment of his enemies, and was content. "Chaste as paper," he wrote, "sober as water, eager for devotion as a communicant, inoffensive as a martyr, I am not displeased to masquerade as a monster of debauchery, a drunkard, a blasphemer and an assassin." And in this noble pride of spirit he forgot the wanton insult to his genius, and by this the world is forgetting it also.

So the magistrate would usurp the world of intelligence, and cramp genius to fit his own Procrustean code, believing that a supremacy in the courts endows him with the control of imagination. But the triumph of to-day becomes the disgrace of to-morrow, and prays for oblivion. On the one side are arrayed "the dissembling and counterfeit saints, demure lookers, hypocrites, pretended zealots, rough friars, buskin monks, and other such sects of men who disguise themselves like maskers to deceive the world." On the other side fight the honest fellows, lovers of merriment and all good things, the frank, the free, the courageous, who esteem beauty above prejudice, and who know that there are a thousand kingdoms whereof the magistrate does not dream. And if for a while the magistrate has his way, they win who deserve the victory. For frankness at the last conquers its opponents, and though its champions fall by the way the cause knows not the ignominy of ultimate failure. In truth it is frankness not "immorality," which the people fear—frankness in whatever guise it presents itself. Now, it is the frankness of revelation that is condemned, that spirit of curiosity which would uncover all things to the lantern of art; now, it is the frankness of intelligence which is thrust into prison, that frankness which would tell the truth even in the face of the ballot-box. So it was that Edgar Poe fell upon misfortune. Not content with picturing new worlds of fancy and humour, not content with winning the realm of mystery for literature, he did not shrink from speaking out to a country submerged in commerce, and miserably he paid the penalty of his misdeeds. Had he not been a critic, to whom prevarication was a cardinal sin, America in her pride might have called him blessed, and rewarded him with her opulent approval. But a habit of candour persuaded him to tell his countrymen the truth, and he fell a victim to the common hatred which might in another hemisphere have ruined Congreve and Baudelaire.

But license, also, must obey the laws of its being, the more stringent, because an infraction leads to the greater infamy. And thus we contemplate the other side of the question. The lighthearted and sincere remain beyond reproach, so long as they find their justification in literature, so long as they are enveloped in the strange atmosphere and live in the false world of romance. But once they reveal their purpose, once they smile self-consciously at their own bravery, they are detestable. If the obscene be sentimental, if it address itself to any other than the artistic sense, it is instantly condemned. There is no essential difference between the Marquis de Sade and the leader of a revival meeting. Each attempts to arouse a false sentiment by illicit means; each would hit its victim below the belt of reason. In either case no appeal is made to the intelligence. The maniac, whether he be pornagraphist or preacher, is anxious to do something, good or bad; and this very anxiety to "do something" renders him suspect. But it is not the magistrate who may play the critic; it is the critic who should play the magistrate. For the right and wrong of literature must be decided by the law, not of the land but of taste. Rabelais, if he have the mind, is free of the world's vocabulary; Dunbar, when he would flyte an enemy, may decorate his speech with what exotic flowers he can find in his fancy's hedgerow. But when the realist, with no better excuse than to satisfy his pedantry, collects a heap of dull irrelevancies, then he pleads guilty to impropriety. For he offends not against morality, but against the law of his art. Accuracy is but a poor defence for the scrupulous ugliness of his choice. "Not to know that a hind has no horns," said Aristotle, "is a less serious matter than to paint it inartistically." And the realist who defends himself from attack on the plea of truth, advances an argument which does not concern his offence. For his is not a sin of outspokenness; he errs in the resolution to unveil secresies, which are merely shocking because they are foreign to the purpose of his romance. Briefly he is no worse than tiresome; yet he owes his notoriety to the general advertisement that he is as daring as Rabelais, as unfettered in his fancy as Petronius himself.

And what of the crooked man, who always detects the immorality of his brother? For him, indeed, shall no excuse be found. His purpose is more infamous than the worst sentimentality, and none has rightly appreciated him save Rabelais, his secular enemy. "Fly from these men," said Alcofribas; "abhor and hate them as much as I do, and upon my faith you will find yourselves the better for it." Furius and Aurelius are their companions; Jeremy Collier and the persecutors of Baudelaire fight disloyally by their side. And to-day, their heirs stand at every street-corner, scratching an advertisement from the revelation of somebody else's "impurity." How well you know them, and their trick of cunning abnegation! If they do give their time to the reading of books, it is not to enjoy them, but rather to hurt the author by some mischievous contrivance. Their sincerity is as doubtful as their wisdom; at the best they can only attract the attention of the prurient to that which he would never have found without guidance; and as they are wont to strip their enemy of his wit before they crucify him, they alone may achieve the harm whereof they would convict others.

In truth, to quote the inspired aphorism of Pascal, "Few men can speak of chastity chastely." And in these words is condemned not only the censorious guardian of his brother, but that unhappy novelist who would cover his freedom with a purpose. There is not, and there can never be, any legitimate purpose in print save pleasure and delight, so that he who would hide his art behind the broken wall of moral excellence is instantly suspected of foul play. When once another intention be admitted than the awakening of sense or intelligence, "moral" or "immoral" matters not a jot. Guilt is confessed in the "purpose," and thereafter the smallest latitude is an outrage upon taste. And so powerful is this cant of shameful latitude condoned by irrelevant aspiration, that the future will not easily escape its tyrannical restriction. But the past at any rate holds a treasury of masterpieces, open and unashamed, which need no concealment for their dignity or their courage. So we may still enjoy a library which arouses the fury and defies the censure of the Puritan. Nor is there any need to close it against the scrutiny of peeping eyes. For genius has locked it, and only intelligence may turn the releasing key.

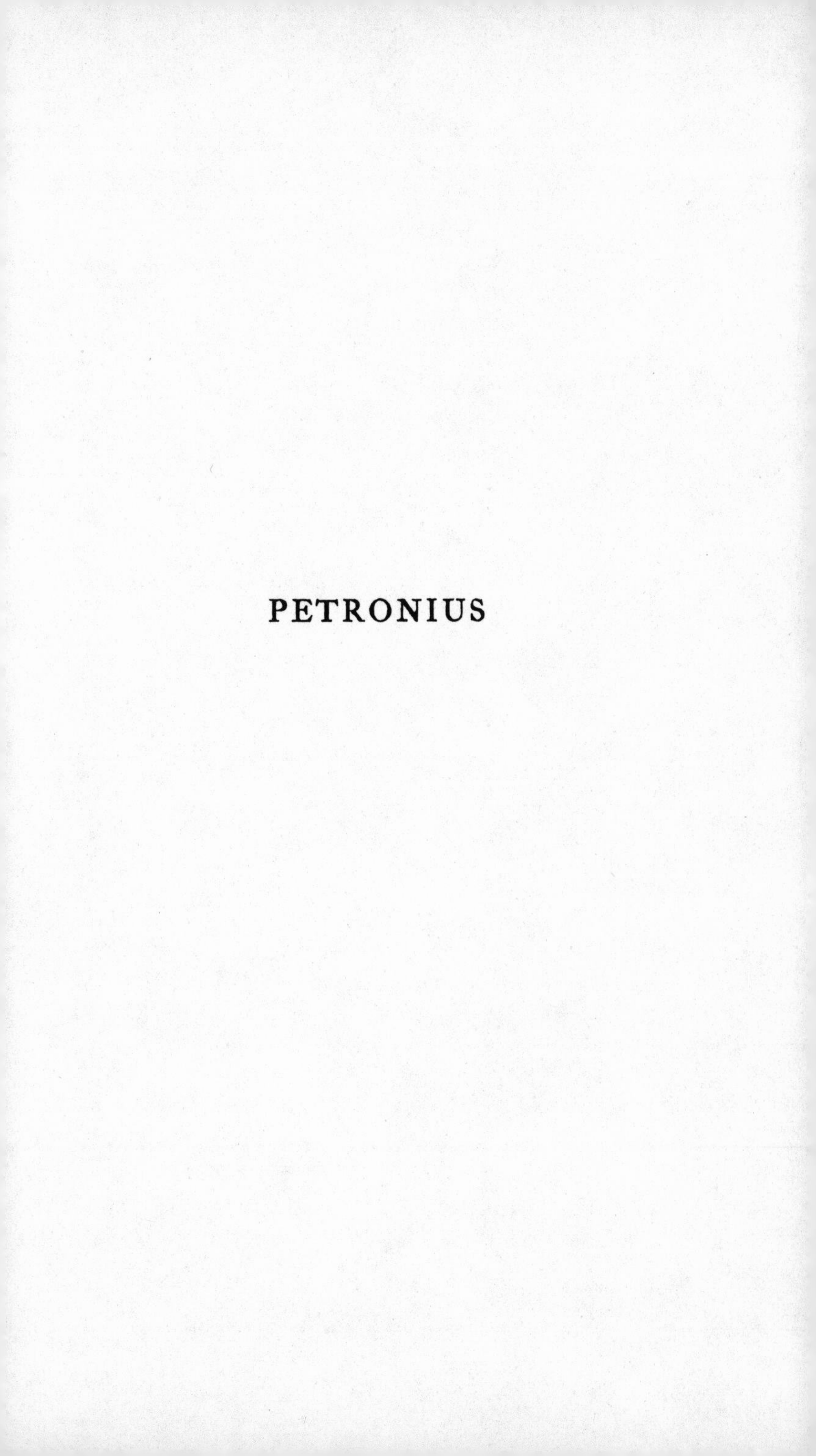

PETRONIUS

PETRONIUS

THE twin enemies of wit—Prudery and Pedantry—have for centuries obscured the proper understanding of Petronius. A chance passage in Tacitus, with the superfluous confusion of a name, long since convinced the scholar that the *Satiricon* was a pamphlet designed for the castigation of Nero, and, when resemblance was lacking, a twisted ingenuity caught glimpses of the dashing Emperor in a common ruffler, a grizzled poet, in the obscene extravagant Trimalchio himself. And while the Pedant was busy torturing a masterpiece out of shape, the Prude averted his eyes in horror lest a spark of brilliant impurity should dazzle him into blindness. But the fear of the Prude is as groundless as the conjecture of the Pedant. The *Satiricon* takes note neither of history nor of morals; it is as remote from ethics as from familiarity. It bids avaunt both the hungry persons, whose inappeasable maw is always avid of moral sustenance, and the sorry scholars, who would leave no jest without its commentary. Petronius, in brief, speaks only to the sincere and the well-disposed; he says no word to those miscreants who would overwhelm wit and gaiety with an infamous suspicion.

The *Satiricon* has one restraining motive: entertainment within the bounds of art. To other fetters it is as resentful as the winds or sea. Not even the learned Teuton, who discovered its controlling subject to be the wrath of Priapus, was justified of his wit. Ingenious as is the fancy, it still lays too heavy a chain upon this wayward, irresponsible Odyssey. No more can be said than that the work of Petronius is a prose epic, the epic (if you will) of the beggar student. Though we know it only in fragments we are confident that its end was as gay a hazard as its beginning: it opened as its author chose, it closed in obedience to the same imaginative will. The bland childhood of the world thrilled at the epic as Homer knew it: the austere nobility of men who were half gods, and of gods who were wholly men, delighted the temper of those too simple to take other than a large view. Even Virgil, with a more conscious art, captured an audience of worshippers, but with him died the love of grandiose types and giant machinery. An age which was curious and introspective demanded an observation which was more precise, more personal; and Petronius, choosing prose for his medium, a prose which was lightened by incomparable interludes of verse, threw a gossamer bridge from the old world to the new. Call it what you will—epic or romance—set over it whatever deity satisfies your whim—Fortuna or Priapus—the *Satiricon* is the gayest, the most light-hearted invention which ever revolutionised the taste and the aspiration of an epoch.

Its heroes are beggars all, beggars draggle-tailed and out-at-elbows. No worse ruffians than the immortal trio—Encolpios, Ascyltos, and Giton—ever took to the highway. They knew neither finery nor self-respect; to-morrow's goal was as far from them as a life's ambition. They wandered under the sun, or sought the discreet encouragement of the stars with that easy conscience which comes of undetected villainy. Home was as strange to them as a change of linen; they journeyed from inn to inn; and they were lucky if, after an evening's debauch, they found their resting-place, or escaped a brawl and a beating. When Encolpios lost himself in the market-place of some nameless city, he provoked a beldame to laughter with the polite question: "Do you know where I have found a lodging for the night?" And after the memorable feast at the house of their patron, Trimalchio, fuddled with wine and luxury, they would have lost their unaccustomed way had not the cunning Giton blazed the posts which should lead to their retreat. Oftentimes, too, when they crawled back from some masterpiece of wickedness, they knew no rest but fisticuffs. "Are you drunk or runaways?" asked the landlord on a celebrated occasion, and there followed a frantic duel between an earthen jar and a wooden candlestick. No trick of gain, no weapon of offence came amiss to the miscreants; and thus they robbed and fought through the breadth and length of

Southern Italy. When they had money they sewed it into the seams of a threadbare tunic, and when they had none they made not the smallest scruple of theft.

Nowhere did they encounter a luckier adventure than at the nocturnal market. They had had the ill-luck to lose their whole fortune in a wood, that fortune which was stitched into an ancient garment. But, in revenge, they had stolen, these beggar students, an elegant and valuable mantle. No sooner had they entered the forum, under the safeguard of night, than they met a ruffian with their lost tunic on his back, and, creeping behind the thief, they presently discovered that their little hoard lurked safe within the seams. Encolpios, himself red-handed, was for having the law of the offender; but Ascyltos, who more prudently trembled at the sight of a policeman, gave his vote for strategy. "Let us buy back the treasure," said he, "rather than embroil ourselves in a troublesome suit." But unhappily two small pieces alone were left in the locker, and these were destined for the purchase of pulse, that hunger might be deferred another day. So there was naught for it but the sale of the stolen mantle. Straightway they displayed their treasure to the admiration of the crowd: but it was instantly recognised, and the ominous shout of "Thieves! thieves!" was raised. The brazen adventurers flung down their prize, and avowed themselves willing to take in exchange the battered tunic. Thereupon a brace of hungry lawyers intervened, urging the sequestration of tunic and mantle, but a scoundrel who hung about the courts clung to the more splendid garment, and our adventurers managed to smuggle the ragged tunic to their lodging.

Thus they wander the world up and down, blatant and unashamed. There is no disaster but falls upon their back; yet they make light of all things with an imperturbable serenity, and leap lightly from crime to crime. They account no dishonour too heavy to be borne; they are flogged and outraged at every turn; but the chance of a meal or of a full pocket heartens them at once, and they are quick indeed to forget an insult. Careless as they are, indifferent as they profess themselves to the misery of the morrow, ill luck pursues them with a persistent and tireless devotion. When to escape from a present evil they go on shipboard, it is not surprising that they find themselves face to face with Lichas and Tryphæna, the prime authors of their misfortune. No disguise is effectual against their enemies. They shave their heads and eyebrows, only to disturb the superstition of a seasick passenger, who denounces them for the unlawful act of clipping their hair, when the winds and waves are at variance. Instantly Lichas recognises them by their voices, and heaven knows what would have been the embroilment, had not shipwreck interrupted a thousand threats of suicide, reconciliation, and revenge.

And who are they, these marvellous beggars, whom Petronius bade to tramp from Cumæ to Naples, and then transported over sea to the hapless

Crotona? Blackguards and scholars all. First there is Encolpios, upon whose tongue the narrative is hung, a scoundrel apt for any cheat, for any effrontery. He is the cleverest and pluckiest of a craven crew. His villainy is checked by no scruple of conscience or tradition. His virtue—if he ever knew it—is torn, like his coat, into ribbons. His life has been passed in many a dishonest shift; once he was a gladiator (so says his friend), but he escaped from the arena, and thereafter murdered his host, who had shown him naught save kindness. What wonder is it, then, that he finds himself a fugitive and an outlaw in a far city of Magna Græcia? What wonder is it that his chosen companions are the victims of nameless vice and unutterable crime? Once, in his sordid career, this pillager of temples, this breaker of friendly houses, sits and deplores his fate in an access of genuine remorse. But it is not his wickedness that irks him: upon that he would smile and smile and be content. He regrets only that he is deserted by the execrable Giton, and presently, buckling his sword at his side, he rushes into the street intent upon vengeance. No sooner, however, is he abroad than a soldier confronts him, demanding the name of his legion and his centurion. And the ready lie that leaps to Encolpios' lips might have saved him had he not been shod like a Greek. "Do the soldiers wear shoes in your army?" asks the guardian of the peace, bidding the ragamuffin lay down his arms. And Encolpios, who dares as much as any man this side cowardice, sorrowfully obeys. For even under the happiest circumstances he is a miracle of poltroonery. When Habinnas, the freedman, enters Trimalchio's banqueting hall, Encolpios takes him for a prætor, and shudders, in his cups, at the imagined majesty of law. At sight of the infamous Quartilla he turns colder than a winter in Gaul, and there is no adventure from which he emerges without a beating. In fact he is flogged as soundly and as often as the fool in a comedy, nor dare he ever resent the perpetual dusting of his threadbare jacket. It was not his to complain. "Ego vapulo tantum" is doubtless his amiable comment upon each fresh outrage, since there is no emergency which he does not fit with a classical allusion.

For this scoundrel Ascyltos is a fit companion. A runaway slave, he, too, has stained his hands with countless crimes, and seeks a discreet oblivion in a wandering life. A bully, as well as a coward, he shares the fears, and the vices, of his friend ; he, too, trembles at the approach of authority ; nor is he ever so happy as when he may sponge a dinner. In evil-doing he knows neither scruple nor hesitation so long as he can pit strategy against force, and when he takes the road with Encolpios he recks as little of his villainy as of his rags. These rapscallions, then, with the infamous Giton, are the real heroes of the *Satiricon*, and thus the beggar-students make their first entrance upon the stage of literature. They would steal in the morning, that at night they might prate the more fluently of poetry and eloquence. No mischief makes them unmindful of their erudition. "We are men of culture," says Encolpios with pride, forgetting for an instant his ragged tunic. They pack their discourse with quip and quotation ; tags from Virgil are ever at their tongue-tip ; and when Encolpios straps the miscreant Giton beneath his bed, he is reminded perforce of Ulysses under the belly of the Cyclops' ram. As they loaf in the market-place of some strange city, or wander in search of plunder along the highway, they will join company with the first-comer, if only he vaunt his learning or profess a pretty taste in poetry.

Thus it is they encounter Agamemnon, the type of the cunning and voluble rhetorician. At the outset he dazzles them with a trite harangue upon the decay of forensic eloquence, and concludes with a foolish copy of verses in the Lucilian manner. But if his knowledge is skin-deep, his villainy reaches his very marrow. In rascality he is a match for his companions, in subtlety he is easily superior ; above all, is he an adept in the art of dining at the rich man's table. He it is, in effect, who brings his ragged companions to the banquet of Trimalchio, and he follows with complete success the twin trades of toady and of bore. Far more amusing and even less reputable is Eumolpos, the ancient poet, whom Encolpios surprises in a picture gallery. His rags proclaim him no friend of the rich, but he has a settled confidence in his own genius, and in season or out he will still recite his intolerable and interminable verses. Poverty and the weight of years have neither broken his spirit nor impaired his gaiety. Not even the fear of death avails to check his volubility, he composes amid the rattle of the storm, and no sooner do they take the road after shipwreck, than he begins to declaim his celebrated epic *The Civil War*. But no man may live by poetry alone, and at Crotona, Eumolpos discovers a brilliant industry in the deception of the legacy-hunters. Now, in that remote city both learning and honesty were held in the lightest esteem. For it was peopled only by the rich who had money to leave, and by the greedy poor who would prey upon inheritances. By a humorous fancy none but the childless were permitted to enter the theatre or to assume a public office. In this realm of comic opera nobody was more at home than Eumolpos. Posing for the carcase, he clamorously invited the attentions of the crows, and for a while the carcase got the better of the bargain. But though his stratagem gave him a welcome taste of magnificence, misfortune and death overwhelmed him at last, and none would have been readier to declare his discomfiture the proper fortune of war than this braggart poetaster.

With such characters, how should the romance satisfy the sensibility of the Prude? You might as reasonably demand that Encolpios should masquerade in a tie-wig and buckle-shoes as expect the manners of South Kensington in this dissipated Odyssey. A French critic in an admirable phrase once praised the "serene unmorality" of Petronius, and the most scrupulous can do no more than confess that the author of the *Satiricon* did not twist his creatures to suit the standard of the law. Why should he, when the policeman was their hourly dread? No, he bade them wander through a distant colony, rags on their back and a jest on their tongue, troubled only by the fear of hunger and the gaol. Villon is of their company: gladly would they have cracked a quart with him, gladly would they have replied to his verses with *ballades* of their own. The heroes of picaresque romance—Gil Blas and Guzman and Lazarillo—are their sworn brethren, and so enduring is the type of the beggar-student that you may meet Encolpios to-day without surprise or misunderstanding.

He haunts the bars of the Strand, or hides him in the dismal alleys of Gray's Inn Road. One there was (one of how many!) who, after a brilliant career at the University, found the highway his natural home, and forthwith deserted the groves of learning for the common hedgerow of adventure. The race-course knew him, and the pavement of London; blacklegs and touts were his chosen companions; now and again he would appear among his old associates, and enjoy a taste of Trimalchio's banquet, complaining the while that the money spent on his appetite might have been better employed in the backing of horses. Though long since he forgot he was a gentleman, he always remembered that he was a scholar, and, despite his drunken blackguardism, he still took refuge in Horace from the grime and squalor of his favourite career. Not long since he was discovered in a cellar, hungry and dishevelled; a tallow candle crammed into a beer-bottle was his only light; yet so reckless was his irresponsibility that he forgot his pinched belly and his ragged coat, and sat on the stone floor, reciting Virgil to another of his profession. Thus, if you doubt the essential truth of Petronius, you may see his grim comedy enacted every day, and the reflection is forced upon you that Encolpios will roam the streets so long as poetry keeps her devotees, and scholarship throws a glamour over idle penury.

Petronius, then, who has been accused of satirising Nero, says no word of Courts or of the great world. He writes as though politics were an extinct science, as though he deemed the earth the ruffler's proper inheritance. Yet in revenge, his most brilliant episode is a parody of magnificence. The *Banquet of Trimalchio* is, to be sure, the reverse of the medal, but nowhere in literature has vulgar display been treated with so genial a humour. So long as print and paper can confer immortality, so long Trimalchio will remain the supreme type of the Beggar on Horseback. The machinery is admirable: the wooden hen sitting upon paste eggs, each of which contains a stuffed ortolan; the Signs of the Zodiac, with their proper dishes; the huge boar, out of which flies a flock of birds—these are inventions in futile extravagance, which correspond completely to the freedman's pompous views of luxury. But far better even than the machinery are the host and hostess. To have drawn two such characters in an age preoccupied with the abstract and the impersonal was a triumph of art, and Petronius has no cause to haggle for his sovereignty.

The very entrance of Trimalchio is a masterpiece: no sooner are you presented with the sketch of the bald man playing tennis and the mob of long-haired boys than you are convinced of the author's quick wit and vivid imagination. Trimalchio's, indeed, is the heroism of wealth: he would as soon pick up a ball which had fallen to the ground as use a silver dish which the clumsiness of a slave has permitted to touch the dust. No wonder he has a timepiece in his hall, and a trumpeter to remind him of the flight of time. His wine is superb. Does not a contemporary label remind the connoisseur that it is Opimian Falernian bottled a hundred years ago? The beggar students could not have found a house better suited to their extravagant taste; their greed renders them easily obsequious; and at the recital of Trimalchio's grandeur their hungry mouths gape wider and wider. He owns as much land as a kite can fly over; he buys nothing, since everything is grown at home; he recks neither of expense nor distance; he sends to Attica that he may improve his bees, and the seeds from which his mushrooms are grown were fetched from the Indies. As he cannot recognise one-tenth of his slaves, so he knows neither the boundaries nor the names of his vast possessions, and he is consumed with anger when a slave announces a newly-acquired and unadvertised estate.

His arrogance is as boundless as his wealth, and he treats his guests with a fine mixture of patronage and effrontery. "Be merry," says he complacently; "once I was no better off than you, but by my own industry I am what I am." He reserves the place of honour for himself, tells the poor devils who gorge at his table that, though they are less distinguished than yesterday's party, they are drinking better wine, and only permits the conversation to grow friendly or casual when it suits his royal fancy. Of wit he has not a touch, but he lightens the gloom with flashes of boorish humour, and his table-talk is a perfect epitome of slavish intelligence. Above all, he delights in verbal puns, and it is his most brilliant sally to call his carver "Carpe," that one word may be both summons and command. The Signs of the Zodiac provoke him to a profound dissertation, and not without a sense of fun he declares that under the Archer are born the cross-eyed scoundrels who stare at the cabbage and steal the bacon. Of the arts he has but a poor opinion, confessing that he cares for nothing but acrobats and trumpeters, and he further avows that, though he did once buy a company of comedians, he only allowed them to play Punch and Judy. At the same time he would be a patron of literature, and he brags for his friends' benefit that he has two libraries, the one of Greek books, the other of Latin. He has even studied declamation, and pertinently asks Agamemnon the subject of the day's controversy. "A poor man and a rich were once at enmity," begins Agamemnon, whereupon Trimalchio, rising to the very summit of his colossal impudence, asks: "What is a poor man?" His taste for poetry has persuaded him to confuse history and legend. He places Hannibal at the siege of Troy, and with the splendid ignorance of a self-neglected man he confuses Medea with Cassandra, and never dreams for a moment that the ruffians, whose momentary admiration he purchases with a meal, are laughing in their sleeves.

Not content with these experiments, he recites some verses of his own composition, compares Cicero and Publius in a lucid criticism, and presently, at a convenient pause, discusses which, after literature, are the most difficult professions. These he pronounces with a pompous security to be medicine and money-changing—medicine, because the doctor can look inside us, and money-changing, because the professor can see bronze through the silver. As the wine goes round, the monumental arrogance of Trimalchio receives its last embellishment. Believing himself almost divine, the freedman has his will read, and even recites his own epitaph, wherein he is described as one who never listened to a philosopher. Happily Habinnas, the maker of tombstones, is present, and he can take for the thousandth time the last dying commands of his patron. But the scene of aggrandisement is disturbed by a quarrel which breaks out suddenly between Trimalchio and his consort, who throws the last words of abuse in her lord's face, and receives by way of guerdon a cup flung at her head and the very lees of obloquy. Finally, Trimalchio devises the supreme punishment, which shall be commensurate with her offence. "Habinnas," he says, "do not put this woman's statue upon my tomb." And, as though this misery were insufficient, "Take care," he adds, "that she be not permitted to kiss my corpse!"

Nor even here shall you find the climax of monstrous stupidity. No sooner is the proper vengeance designed Fortunata than Trimalchio contrives another masterpiece of vanity. He rehearses with a perfect realism his own funeral. Lying in state, he bids the trumpeters blow, and exacts from his friends a tribute of interested praise. But the trumpeters blow to such purpose, that the watchmen burst into the house, fearing a fire, and in the confusion the drunken beggars make their escape, to pursue with a gay heart and a tempered magnificence their ancient professions of vagabondage and thievery.

The portrait of Trimalchio is a triumph of realism. Yet none the less, it is of heroical proportions. Its grandeur and loftiness are, at least, as remarkable as its pitiless veracity. Here, in fact, is a new element in literature: truth cast in a large and epic mould. You laugh at the freedman's extravagance, but your laughter lags behind your admiration, and you feel that you are confronted by the inverse of some vast deity. Fortunata, on the other hand, is more intimate and more modern. She is burnt into the page with a grotesque certainty that suggests an etching by Goya, and being less heroically designed, she is more personal, more living than Trimalchio himself. He is the luck of the household, she the brain. She counts her money by the bushel, and nothing escapes her that concerns her lord or his possessions. Obscure as she is, and ill-born, she rules him with a word, and if she says it is dark at noonday, he lights the lamp. But his faith puts no check on her loyalty, and no drop of water moistens her lips until the household is at peace. She counts the silver, she divides the broken meats among the slaves, and then, and not till then, will she sit down to dinner, or believe herself the equal of her husband. Yet, in her hours of ease, she is not without accomplishments ; she will dance the *cordax*, that marvel of impropriety, against the whole world, and she has a perfect talent for scurrility. When Habinnas and his horrible wife Scintilla arrive at Trimalchio's feast from a funeral, Fortunata is nowhere to be seen. Forthwith the slaves are bidden to call her, and four times her name is shouted. She enters in all her squalid finery, wiping her hands on the handkerchief round her neck ; her slippers are laced with gold, and corded buskins show beneath her gown, which is cherry-coloured and girdled with green. Forthwith she mumbles affectionately to Scintilla, and the good-humoured ladies brag to each other of their vulgar finery.

Fortunata, indeed, is etched by a master, and at the banquet none of the guests fall far below the quality of their hosts. In the absence of Trimalchio they exchange the stock phrases of an impoverished intelligence with a genius of persistence that cannot be matched outside the *Polite Conversation*. They send across the table an endless fire of proverbs and catchwords. They pack their discourse full of the gags of the tavern, as though they were actors preparing for the Saturnalia or a Christmas pantomime. They anticipate Sam Weller with a "better luck next time, as the yokel said when he lost his speckled pig." They slip in a quip or a quirk, alive from the street, at the briefest interruption of wit. They are magnificent, worthless, obscene; but they are never dull, and an evening spent in the blackguard society of these beggar-students passes in a flash of merriment. You meet them with pleasure, you leave them with regret, and only when the author of their being tempts you to curiosity about himself.

For Petronius is as secret as Shakespeare, as impersonal as Flaubert. If he has crammed his book with the fruits of a liberal experience, he has resolutely suppressed himself. Whether or no he be the Petronius of the *Annals* is uncertain and indifferent. Most assuredly the author of the *Satiricon* would have hated the brutality of Tigellinus and despised the taste of Nero, that Imperial Amateur. But history is silent, and conjecture is a mule. Wherefore we know him only as the writer of an incomparable romance, which has no other motive than amusement, and no better virtues than gaiety and lightheartedness. The masterpiece, as we have it to-day, is but a collection of fragments, but its composition is not impaired by incompleteness, and there is scarce a fragment which is not perfect in itself. For Petronius had the true genius of the story-teller: his openings are as direct as if silhouetted in black upon a white sheet. Before all the ancients, he had a sense of background; he knew precisely what space his figures would occupy; and he never permitted a wanton exaggeration or a purposeless perversion. The material of his romance was the squalid life of his age, by land and by sea, by day and by night, in the close town and under the large air of heaven. He was a very prince of intelligence; he understood as acutely as he observed, and nothing escaped either mind or eye. His courage, moreover, was equal to his understanding: he never shrank from laying violent hands upon truth; he turned life inside out with a very passion of fearlessness.

The first among the ancients to cultivate the gift of curious characterisation, he invented a set of personages, who are not only types but living men. He handled the sorcery and superstition of his age with a skill which not even Apuleius might excel, and for all his levity he knew how to strike the reader with horror. Moreover, he was an adept at the Milesian Fable, a haunting form of literature which eludes the most diligent research; and the *Story of the Ephesian Widow*, which even Jeremy

Taylor does not disdain to quote, is the very model of its kind, and withal the perfection of ironic humour. Nor does this complete the tale of his perfections: he was as accomplished a critic as antiquity can show. His parody of Lucan is a dissertation upon the art of poetry; the reflections which precede it are a miracle of insight; and what praise need you bestow upon the man who first discovered in *Horace* a "curiosa felicitas"?

Who was he? What was he? Whence came he? These questions must remain for ever without an answer. One thing only is certain, he was a gentleman, and incomparably aristocratic. He stood a creator, high above the puppets of his creation, and in nothing does he show his greatness so admirably as in the serene aloofness of his temperament. One Petronius, surnamed *Arbiter Elegantiarum*, broke two Murrhine vases envied by an Emperor, and when, driven to suicide, he opened a vein, he stopped the blood, so long as the converse of his friends was an entertainment. The author of the *Satiricon* was capable of both these actions, and an age is rich indeed that produced two such heroes. But no more may be said save that he revealed himself a classic and the friend of tradition. In the very act to invent a new literature, he quoted Virgil and Horace with an admirable devotion; he wrote a prose so pure and simple that even the flashes of slang and popular speech wherewith it is illuminated do not interrupt its high tranquillity. We may yet discover another fragment of his priceless work : we are never likely to pierce the mystery of his being. But we are content to look upon him as a great gentleman, and to acknowledge that under his auspices we would rather dine with Trimalchio and his rapscallions than with Lucullus himself.

HELIODORUS

HELIODORUS *

HELIODORUS, Bishop of Tricca, bidden to choose between the prelacy and his *Æthiopica*, rather suffered the deprivation of his title than "lose the glory of so excellent piece." Such is the one poor legend which serves Heliodorus for a biography. Nor may it claim the honour of antiquity, since, though in modern times it has never lacked appreciative iteration, its invention is no older than Nicephorus Callistus and the fourteenth century. Translated into all modern tongues, this unsupported testimony has aroused an admiration for Heliodorus in the breasts of thousands for whom the *Æthiopica* is merely Greek, and who have scarce heard, even at second hand, of the loves of Theagenes and Chariclia. From Montaigne † the fable

* An Æthiopian Historie, written in Greeke by Heliodorus, no lesse wittie than pleasaunt. Englished by T. Underdowne, and newly corrected and augmented with divers and sundrie new additions by the said Authour. Imprinted by F. Coldocke. London. 1587.

† "Heliodorus, ce bon evesque de Tricca," thus runs the passage, "ayma mieulx perdre la dignité, le profit, la devotion, d'une prelature si venerable, que de perdre sa fille, fille qui dure encore bien gentille, mais, à l'aventure pourtant un peu trop curieusement et mollement goderonnée, pour fille ecclesiastique et sacerdotale, et de trop amoureuse façon."

crept into Burton's *Anatomy*, and thence into every treasury of the commonplace, until, industriously repeated, it has become more true than truth itself. And yet, like truth itself, it is manifestly difficult of belief. For, in Montaigne's despite, the *Æthiopica* is a work of which the most exalted bishop might be proud. In one aspect it is nothing less than a panegyric of chastity—a Joseph Andrews stripped of its satire. And should not the bishop rather enjoy promotion for so conspicuous a service than witness the destruction of his solitary child? Nor does Heliodorus stand in need of any false dignity, since his style and description, devised, as an epilogue, by himself, are far more honourable than the title bestowed of Nicephorus: "Thus endeth the Æthiopian historie of Theagenes and Chariclia," you read on the last page, "the authour whereof is Heliodorus of Emesos, a citie in Phœnicia, sonne of Theodosius, which fetched his petigree from the Sunne."* Who would not rather boast a descent direct from the Sun, than sit in far-off Thessaly upon the throne of Tricca? But Nicephorus Callistus had thus much support for his ingenious fiction, that Socrates, an ecclesiastical writer of the fifth century, gave the see of Tricca to one Heliodorus. Nevertheless, similarity of name is poor evidence, and until you desert the author for his work you may believe whatever legend you will.

* *τοίονδε πέρας ἔσχε τὸ σύνταγμα τῶν περὶ Θεαγένην καὶ Χαρίκλειαν Αἰθιοπικῶν· ὃ συνέταξεν ἀνὴρ Φοίνιξ Ἐμεσηνὸς, τῶν ἀφ' Ἡλίου γένος, Θεοδοσίου παῖς Ἡλιόδωρος.*

The *Æthiopica* is the forerunner of the modern Romance, the ancestor in a direct line of the Novel of Adventure. The invention of Heliodorus carries the reader far away from life and observation. Blood-thirsty pirates and armed men, caves and ambushes, dreams and visions, burnings, poisonings, and sudden deaths, battle and rapine—these are the material of his ancient story. It has been called a prose epic ; yet it is more nearly related to *Ivanhoe* than to the *Iliad*. There is no artifice of the "historical novel" which Heliodorus does not anticipate. The challenge thrown down in his Fourth Book by "one of goodly person-age and of greate courage" might have been devised by Sir Walter himself, and the miraculous escapes of the hero and heroine are still the commonplaces of popular fiction. But the chastity of Chariclia, the more than human control of Theagenes, are of the author's own contriving ; and these qualities most assuredly give character and consistency to his narra-tive. It is in his opening scene that Heliodorus best approves his skill. He plunges at once into a very tangle of events, and captures the attention by a fear-less contempt of prologue and explanation. "As soone as the day appeared," to quote Underdowne's picturesquely inaccurate version, "and the Sunne began to shine on the tops of the hilles, men whose custome was to live by rapine and violence ranne to the top of a hill that stretched towards the mouth of Nylus, called Heracleot : where standing awhile they viewed the sea underneath them, and when they had looked a good season a far off into the same, and could see nothing that might put them in hope of pray, they cast their eyes somewhat neare the shoare: where a shippe, tyed with cables to the maine land, lay at road, without sailers, and full fraughted, which thing, they who were a farre of might easily conjecture: for the burden caused the shippe to drawe water within the bourdes of the decke." And when a maid, "endued with excellent beauty," is pictured gazing upon a sorely wounded youth, the reader knows forthwith what is in store for him, and foresees the happy end of a familiar embroilment. Throughout the author shows himself a master of construction. Though his plot be involved, though his story begin anywhere else than at the beginning, it is the surest of hands which holds the threads. The countless misfortunes which befall the actors of the melodrama, before ever the thieves of Egypt carry away their prey, are set forth in a series of episodes, which gives the book an appearance of separate stories lightly held together. No fresh personage comes upon the scene but he proceeds to divulge the adventures of the past. Thus Cnemon relates the story of Demeneta, his jealous stepmother, an invention worthy the genius of Boccaccio; thus Calasiris, that blameless old man, true descendant of the Tragic Chorus, only begetter of unnumbered Old Adams, recounts his own mishaps with peevish tediousness, adding thereto the early history of Chariclia and Theagenes; thus you are told how Chariclia, exposed to doubtful fortune, was committed, jewels and all, to Charicles, and how Theagenes went forth from Thessaly to perform the funeral rites of Pyrrhus, son of Achilles. Yet, despite this constant doubling back to the past, the purpose of the narrative is never confused, and you reach the appointed end with a complete consciousness of the story's shape and construction. To-day the artifice seems simple enough. The personages of the romance are known to one another by token or by recollection at the first encounter, until the effect savours rather of modern farce and the strawberry mark than of the pitiless self-discovery of Œdipus. But the trick might well have showed a miracle of ingenuity in the fourth century; nor does Heliodorus pretend either to Sophoclean irony or to the compact development of Athenian tragedy. In brief, he tells a discursive story of love and capture, and tells it to such purpose that his very faults have served for an example to centuries of romance.

For him the adventure was the beginning and the end of art. His book contains scarce a hint of character, and he wove his vast tapestry from the plays and epics of Greece without a glance thrown on the life of his time. Wherefore his *Æthiopica* belongs to no period and to no country. It is as remote from reality as the *Arcadia*—of which, perchance, it was an inspiration—or the other dead romances of the Elizabethans. For Heliodorus Egypt and Thessaly are names and no more; his personages fight and love, are captured and set free in an age which is heroic despite its complications. The motives which persuade Theagenes and Chariclia to their intervals of activity are of the simplest. No subtlety ever disturbs the logical result of hate or jealousy; not one creation submits to an individual impulse. Each has his qualities, each acts or suffers, not as in a real world but as in a world of phantasy, wherein Heliodorus pulls the strings. Now and again the novelist is surprised into a piece of observation, the more strange for its very rarity: for instance, Arsinoe is despised of Nausikles, "because that while she sang her cheekes swelled, and were unseemly, and her eyes stared, almost leaving their accustomed place."* Not a miracle of insight, truly, but a patch of vivid relief upon a pallid picture. The deaf fisherman, too, whom Calasiris (in Book v.) finds mending his nets, is a sketch fashioned from memory or a notebook, and is free from the prevailing taint of the heroic. "After I had gone a little way," thus Underdowne, "I sawe an olde man which was a fisher, that satte mending his broken nettes, before his doore. I came to him, and saide, Goode man, God save you, and tell me I pray you, where a man may gette lodging? He answered me: it was rent upon a promontorie hereby: being lette slippe upon a rock, which they sawe not. I aske not that, quoth I, but you shall show us great courtesie, if either you yourselfe wilbe our hoste, or else shewe us some other Inne.

* The Greek is more obviously realistic than Underdowne's English. Here it is: *ἐπειδὴ κυρτουμένην αὐτῇ τὴν παρειὰν ἐν τοῖς αὐλήμασι εἶδε, καὶ πρὸς τό βίαιον τῶν φυσημάτων ἀπρεπέστερον ἐπὶ τὰς ῥῖνας ἀνισταμένην, τό τε ὄμμα πιμπράμενον καὶ τῆς οἰκείας ἕδρας ἐξωθούμενον.*

He answeared, not I, for I was not aborde with them." But this cross-purpose is not characteristic: it seems to have crept by stealth into an impersonal narrative. Again, Heliodorus is curiously insensitive to landscape: a failing the more noteworthy since the author of the incomparable *Daphnis and Chloe* was doubtless his near contemporary. You journey with Chariclia from Egypt into Thessaly; with Cnemon you wander to the Peiraeus; but the impression of atmosphere is faint indeed. If the long, low banks of the Nile compel the writer's interest, if he have some vague sense of marshland, he caught it not from life but from Herodotus; and Underdowne's phrase, "When all was whishte in the marish," is infinitely more expressive than the original Greek: *σιγῆς δὲ τὸ ἕλος κατασχούσης*.

But, though we know not whether Heliodorus were Bishop of Tricca or descendant of the Sun, his book assures us more certainly than the word of all the Fathers that he was a lettered recluse, who sought in books the experience which life denied him. There was never a writer who closed his senses more resolutely to the sights and sounds of the world. In him the faculty of observation was replaced by the self-consciousness of the student. Not even his vocabulary was fresh or original. Coray, the wisest of his editors, has proved that he borrowed his words as ingeniously as he concocted his episodes. His prose, in fact, is elaborately composed of tags from Homer and the Tragedians. It is as though an English novelist should establish his diction upon a study of Chaucer and the Elizabethan drama! There results the style of a bookworm, not even remotely poetical, but broken by inapposite echoes of all the poets. To turn from Heliodorus to Longus is to change a clever craftsman for a finished artist. For Longus played upon language as upon a various and subtle instrument, calling therefrom harmonies unknown before, and it is the misfortune of Heliodorus that time and subject compel a comparison of the *Æthiopica* with *Daphnis and Chloe*, indisputably the greatest of Greek romances.

One other habit determines the writer of culture: a delight in commonplace and in the improvement of the occasion. He will always point a moral, if he do not thereby adorn his tale. "Such is the appearance of very nobilitie," you read in the English of Underdowne, "and the force of comeliness, which can subdue the disposition of theeves, and bring under the wilde and savage." The reflection may be matched for triteness where you will. But when Heliodorus calls upon Calasiris to prove that Homer was an Egyptian, he approaches still more nearly the Barlovian ideal, and when the irreproachable Calasiris replies to Cnemon's entreaty: "Although it be nothing neare to our purpose to talk of such things, yet I will briefly tell you:" you expect a vision of Harry Sandford. However, if Heliodorus wrote the prose of a bookworm, if he looked for life rather on his shelves than in the market-place, if the love of Theagenes and Chariclia be the milk-and-water of passion, the passion, indeed, of Paul and Virginia, his invention is beyond reproach, and an age which prefers insight before fancy may still admire the *Æthiopica* as the beginning of romance.

The popularity of Heliodorus was early established. His masterpiece has been translated into many tongues. Nor has it proved a mere solace and inspiration: there is a legend that in the sixteenth century it was gravely considered a handbook of tactics. In 1534 the *Editio Princeps** appeared, and seventeen years later an adventurous Pole, one Stanislaus Warschewiczki, turned it into plain and serviceable Latin.† The preface, which is dated 'Ex Warschewiczke, paterno rure, Calendas Augusti, 1551," gives a human interest to a long-forgotten work. It is strange, indeed, that Heliodorus, travelling betimes to far-off Poland, should have amused the leisure of a territorial lord. But for us the ancient editions have a more than picturesque interest, because they must needs have been in the hands of Thomas Underdowne, the first to English the loves of Theagenes and Chariclia. Unlike Sir Thomas North, Underdowne owed no debt to Amyot, whose *Æthiopica*, published in 1559, is not for an instant comparable to his masterly versions of Plutarch and Longus.

* Heliodori Æthiopicæ Historiæ libri decem, nunquam antea in lucem editi. Basileæ, 1534.

† Thus the book, a noble quarto, is described upon the title-page: Heliodori Æthiopicæ Historiæ libri decem, nunc primum e Græco sermone in Latinum translati. Stanislao Warschewiczki Polono Interpreti. Basileae, 1551.

Prolix and tasteless, it neither represents the original, nor is it worthy on its separate merit. Amyot failed with Heliodorus as Angell Day failed with Longus, and as Amyot turned *Daphnis and Chloe* into a phantasy, beautiful as his original, so Thomas Underdowne converted *Theagenes and Chariclia* from the faded experiment of a studious pedant into a fresh and open-aired romance.

But Underdowne fails as a translator, because his ignorance of Greek and Latin was frank and magnificent. There is no page of him that is not shamed by a childish misunderstanding of the original. That he used the Latin more intimately than the Greek is proved by the fact that he follows the ingenious Warschewiczki into his every error. Indeed, he nowhere declares his acquaintance with Greek, though now and again the ingenuity of his fault suggests that the true text of Heliodorus was in his hands ; while he indirectly acknowledges his debt to the Latin version by translating into characteristic English a brief biography of his author. "In the stile," writes Underdowne, after the Polish scholar, "is much exquisite diligence, yet doth it bring with it a certaine delightful oblectation, united, as is meete in such an Argument, with singular myrth." But, if Underdowne had any sense of his author's style (which is hardly credible), he kept sternly aloof from it. There is no trace in the English version of the Greek writer's foppish pedantry. The style of Underdowne is all unspoiled by inapposite quotation or ingenious illusion, and if it be more truly poetical than the original, that is because a rhythmically cadenced prose is nearer poetry than a bundle of conceits. But he made no attempt to represent his author: by design or accident he got as far from Heliodorus as possible. To compare the two is to wonder that the one has even a distant relation to the other. For so fine is Underdowne's feeling for adventure, so admirable is his local colour, that he gives the story the period and the atmosphere which Heliodorus perforce withheld. With the English in your hand, you lose that uncertainty of time and place which the Greek's vague heroism inspires. You are in the very citadel of Romance; and the citadel is built in Elizabethan England; and the romance is unfolded to you, not in the tasteless phrase thought out by a man of culture in his sombre study, but in a medley of vivid words culled from the chap-books or heard in the market-place. For Underdowne was of those who would put the gods into doublet and hose. His hero is "Captaine Theagenes"; Calasiris addresses Charicles frankly with a "Marry Syr Caricles," while such phrases as "Syr Prieste" and "Jollie Dame" (ὦ θαυμασία) sparkle on every page. The modern tone, as Underdowne understood it, is so scrupulously preserved that you will not find a dozen suggestions of a classical origin in the book. "Tush (quoth she), thy prating is of no effect": thus the old woman Cybele to her son. And when Chariclia stands at the stake, unharmed by the fire, "Arsace, not well in her wits, skipte from the walles, and came out at a posterne with a great company of her guarde." (τὴν δὲ Ἀρσάκην μή καταισχῦνσαν καθαλέσθαι τε ἀπὸ τῶν τειχῶν, καὶ διὰ πυλίδος ἐκδραμοῦσαν σὺν πολλῇ δορυφορίᾳ.) Then, that there may never be a retrogression into antiquity, μουσεῖον appears as "studie," κιθάραν as "Virginalls," and on one occasion Theagenes is seen "walking about the church and in the cloisters." (περὶ τὸν νεὼν καὶ τόν περίβολον.) To resume, Underdowne was a poor translator but a great writer. He had neither the knowledge nor the subtlety to put Heliodorus into an appropriate dress. He did but take the *Æthiopica* for his motive, fashioning thereupon an excellent narrative, which might still be an ensample to writers of romance; and thus he proved that the translator may be above his original, that inaccuracy is no bar to a brilliant "transformation."

As it was Underdowne's supreme ambition to quicken the Greek into the vigorous life of romantic English, he was ever on the outlook for strange and daring words. Μοιχᾶται he converts into "plays the naughtipack," a phrase whose excellent sound and humour are ill warranted by the original. Thus, too, he renders the commonplace μειράκιον by so expressive a word as "princocks," and there is not a sentence that his courage does not improve out of knowledge. "When this affection had *gripped* their hearts, they became pale," he writes of the lovers' meeting; and you realise how picturesque is the English when you turn to the Greek, and find no more than *τοῦ πάθους καὶ τὴν καρδίαν ἐπιδραμόντος, ὠχρίασαν.* With admirable effect, too, does he throw a characteristic word into his sentence: "And therewithal Cariclia glistered at the race ende," though "glistered" finds its suggestion in *ἐξέλαμψεν.* When Calasiris wraps Chariclia's quiver "in a torne and naughty piece of leather" (*τετρυχωμένοις κωδίοις*), it is difficult to explain your delight in the phrase, yet you know that none but an Elizabethan could have written it. And when Underdowne renders *τινὰ τῶν ἀγοραίων*, "one of the makeshifts of the city," or, having no better occasion than *εἰρήνης αὐτοῖς ἐγίνετο πρύτανις*, stumbles upon so ingenious an expansion as "made himself their loveday and peace," it is plain that if he treated his Heliodorus with scant courtesy, at least he knew how to embellish him.

His version, then, is purely English, untouched of Greek or foreign influence. Gifted with an unerring tact of narrative, endowed with a rare sense of rhythm, Underdowne was more than the most of his contemporaries a maker of English prose. In his pages may be found an origin of the Authorised Version. Accustomed to esteem our own Bible a separate masterpiece, we forget that the translators of James's reign were but the heirs of the Elizabethans. The style, which they handled with so fine a bravery, they found fashioned ready to their hand. North and Underdowne, Holland and Adlington, had come before to establish a tradition of distinguished prose. And it is Underdowne who most nearly approaches the august severity of the English Bible. For example, contemplate the following passage: "Wherefore I with wayling beweepe my sorrow, like a Birde, whose nest a dragon pulleth down, and devoureth her young before her face, and is afraid to come nigh, neither can she flee away." Might not these lines be culled from the Psalms or the Prophets? And while Underdowne preserves the dignity and colour of his narrative at this high level, he holds in reserve the power of raising his note, of making his page blare (so to say) with a trumpet call. Thus Theagenes comes before the wanton Arsace to find her habited in splendour: "When he came in and sawe her sittinge in her chaire of estate, clothed in purple and clothe of golde, glorious with jolly jewels, and her costly bonet, finely attyred and decked, with her garde about her, and the chiefe magistrates of the Persians by her, he was not abashed a whit but rather the more incouraged against the Persian braverie." Though the passage bear not the smallest likeness to the thinly accurate Greek, how admirable are its qualities of sound and strength! Or choose another specimen at hazard, and let Underdowne prove himself a master of the picturesque. It is a portrait of Theagenes drawn by Calasiris: "Such brightness did hys sight bring unto us, in as much as he was on horseback also, with a speare of Ashe, poynted with steele in his hande; he had no helmet on, but was bare headed. His cloke was of Purple wrought with Golde, wherein was the battell of the

Centaures and Lapithes: on the button of his cloke was Pallas pictured, bearing a shielde before her breast, wherein was Gorgons head. The comelines and commendation of that which was done was somewhat increased by the easie blowing of the winde, which mooved his haire about his necke, parting it before his forhead, and made his cloake wave, and the nether parts thereof to cover the back and buttocks of his horse. You would have sayde that hys horse did knowe the beautie of his master, and that he beeing very faire himselfe, did beare a passing seemely man, he rayned so, and with pricked up eares, he tossed his head, and rolled his eyes fiercelie, and praunced, and leapt in so fine sort." That is prose of a form and substance which could only have been understood in the fresh childhood of literature. And it is good indeed to contemplate the splendid barbarity of this ancient style in an age when a hatred of affectation, a foolish deference to an attenuated tradition, have replaced every individual characteristic by a precise uniformity.

Such the book upon which Thomas Underdowne has established his claim to the grateful memory of all those who love rich, well-measured English. It is described upon the title-page with characteristic circumstance and completeness. "An Æthiopian Historie," thus runs the edition of 1587, "written in Greeke by Heliodorus, no lesse wittie than pleasaunt. Englished by T. Underdowne, and newly corrected and augmented with divers and sundrie new additions by the said Authour. Imprinted by F. Coldocke.

London. 1587." If we may believe Bliss (in his *Athenæ Oxonienses*), the first edition, which bears no date, was printed for Henrie Wykes by Frances Coldocke in 1577, so that the book had been ten years in the world before it was "newly augmented." The "historie" is dedicated in terms of pomp and flattery to the Right Honourable Edward Deviere, Lord Boulbecke, Earl of Oxenford, Lord Great Chamberlain of England, to whom the author acknowledges himself "not knowen." His choice of a patron is excellently reasoned, being withal a proof of implicit trust in his author. "Now of al knowledge fit for a noble gentleman, I suppose the knowledge of histories is most seeming. For furthering whereof, I have englished a passing fine and witty historye, written in Greeke by Heliodorus, and for right good cause consecrated the same to your honourable Lordship." In the address to the Gentle Reader, which stands by way of preface, the worthy Underdowne is not so wisely guided. He repents him of his folly, and craves pardon for his boldness. Grimly conscious that the stationers' shops are "fullfraughted with books of small price," he confesses that "the looseness of these dayes rather requireth grave exhortations to vertue, than wanton allurements to leudnesse." But the harm being done, he deems it no dishonour to correct the errors wherewith his own or the corrector's negligence has disfigured the pages. His theory of correction is still unintelligible, for no book was ever read for the press with more shameful inaccuracy than this "newly corrected and augmented" edition of 1587. But why insist upon orthography, where you find nobility of style? The translator then excuses the enterprise, which his riper years condemn, on the ground that the book "punisheth the faultes of evill doers, and rewardeth the well livers." "What a king is Hidaspes?" he asks triumphantly. "What a patterne of a good prince? What happy successe had he? Contrariwise. What a leawde woman was Arsace? What a patterne of evill behaviour? What an evill end had shee?" Thus he would ask a superfluous pardon, and excuse a work that needed no defence. And the world is content, readily condoning this slender fault of moral apology, inevitable under Elizabeth, as in the later age of Victoria.

Of Thomas Underdowne's life little enough is certain. The son of Steven Underdowne, he sojourned a while at the University of Oxford. But he left it without a degree; and we know not whether he betook himself to the church or spent a more adventurous life in the courts. His published works provide a scanty knowledge, which we search in vain to supplement. In 1566 there was printed by Rychard Jones a small octavo, little more than a pamphlet, entitled *The Excellent Historie of Theseus and Ariadne*, "written in English Meeter by Thomas Underdowne."* Such was the beginning, and three

* Thus it stands in the Stationers' Registers for 1566: "Recyvyd of Richard Jonnes for his lycense for the prynting of an history, intituled Thesious and Arr(i)adne, iiijd."

years later a more ambitious work was registered at the Stationers' Hall: *Ovid, his invective against Ibis.* "Translated into English Meeter, whereunto is added by the translator, a short draught of all the stories and tales contained therein, very pleasant to read."* On the title-page is no note of authorship; but the dedication, addressed in the common style of adulation to Sir Thomas Sackville, is signed T. U., and the writer avows that he honours Sir Thomas, partly because he is the friend of poets, partly on account of "the good affection your honour hath had to my dear father, Steven Underdowne." The version is of the slenderest merit, for Underdowne was no poet, and the loose rattle of his lines is neither an echo of the Latin nor an original harmony. The Tudor translators, skilled as they were in prose, failed most miserably in the more delicate task of Englishing poetry, while the truth was still undiscovered that in a strange tongue prose is the best equivalent of verse. The incidental lines, which break the march of Heliodorus' narrative, are turned into the merest doggrel:

> To-morrow shalt thou with the maide
> escape Arsaces band:
> And soone be brought with her into
> the Æthiopian land.

* Under 1569 you may read in the Registers: "Recevyd of Thomas e (a)st for his lycense for the pryntynge of a booke intituled OVIDE Invictive againste Ibis . . . iiijd."

This jingle halts for an elegiac couplet, in the eighth book of the *Æthiopica*. But Underdowne had already determined his metre when he laid hands upon the Ibis, and thus he renders Ovid's exquisitely finished verse:

> The Spring with Autumne shalbe one
> with Winter Sommers guyse:
> And in one countrey shall the Sun
> at once both set and yse.
> Ere I will concord have with thee,
> sith thou didst breake the band:
> And set these weapons clean a syde,
> that I have tane in hand.

And not content with thus dishonouring his author, Underdowne bombasts out his book with classical mythology, which, for all its characteristic euphuism, is well-nigh unreadable, and inclines you to believe that, after all, Underdowne was a pedant, who, like Philemon Holland, left Oxford for an usher's stool, and employed a scanty leisure in the Englishing of Latin verse or Greek prose.

Now, this brief record of achievement speaks little of Underdowne's life or character. But the preface to the *Æthiopian Historie* convicts him of a pleasant coquetry with morality, and the notes which adorn his "margent," and which, as the author too sanguinely suggests, "will well supply the want of a table," amply sustain the conviction. For it is in this "margent" that the translator most clearly reveals himself. His erudition is no less obvious than his determination to do good. On every page are such pearls of the commonplace as "Mans life unstable" or "A woman is best at a souden attempt." At times he will quote Seneca, and "Necessitas plus poscit quam pietas solet" is his comment upon Thisbe's hasty burial. Or he will derive instruction for the present from the piety of the past, thus proving his implicit faith in the Æthiopian History. When Calasiris, in love with Rhodopis, "determined not to dishonest the Priesthoode," Underdowne is ready with the admirably trite reflection: "God graunt that the honestie of this heathen priest condemne not some of our ministers which professe the gospel." Is that not written with the very accent of Puritanism? Or he will turn for his sustenance to ancient history, and suggest that Charicles "was perhaps of Themistocles' opinion, who rather chose for his daughter a man without money, than money without a man." But though the notes do not serve "for a table," they prove that Underdowne's instruction was sound as his morality was sincere.

The popularity of the *Æthiopian Historie* is well attested by the great rarity of Underdowne's tiny quarto. The book that drifts to the fishmongers most commonly escapes destruction: it is the chapbook, passed through a thousand hands, that is read into effacement. But there is other testimony that Heliodorus was a favourite from Elizabeth's reign to the close of the seventeenth century. Shakespeare* knew him, and read him, you may be certain, in Underdowne's version. Not a few other translators tried their hand upon him, accentuating by their childish bungling the admirable style and sense of the first version. Abraham Fraunce, for instance, in *The Countess of Pembroke's Yvy Church*,† would parade his scholarship by forcing a fragment of Heliodorus into clumsy hexameters. Of this work Ben Jonson, in a conversation with Drummond of Hawthornden, said the first and last word: "that Abraham Fraunce in his English Hexameters was a fool." Concerning this truth there is no argument, and to read Fraunce's *Beginning of Heliodorus his Æthiopicall History*, is to prefer the unkempt doggrel of Underdowne's interludes. Fortunately the "beginning" only occupies six pages; but the Countess of Pembroke can scarce have appreciated such stuff as this:

> As soone as Sun-beames could once peepe out fro' the
> mountaynes,
> And by the dawne of day had somewhat lightened
> Olympus,

---

* In *Twelfth Night* (Act V. sc. i.) there is a direct reference to *Theagenes and Chariclia.* Says Orsino:

> "Why should I not, had I the heart to do it,
> Like to the Egyptain thief, at point of death,
> Kill what I love?"

† The Countess of Pembroke's Yvy Church. By Abraham Fraunce. London. Printed by Thomas Orwyn, for William Ponsonby, dwelling in Paules Churchyard, at the signe of the Bishop's Head. 1591.

> Men, whose lust was law, whose life was still to be lusting,
> Whose thryving thieving, conveyd themselves to an hil-top,
> That stretched forward to the Heracleotical entry
> And mouth of Nylus : looking thence downe to the maine sea
> For sea-faring men ; but seeing none to be sayling,
> They knew 'twas booteless to be looking there for a booty.

Yes, Abraham Fraunce in his hexameters was a fool. There is not a line that will scan without violence to sense and accent ; and the brief fragment's sole merit is its abrupt termination.

A story less dramatic than *Theagenes and Chariclia* can scarce be imagined. Its essential characteristic is to unfold itself after the manner of an epic. A tangle of episodes, whose chief distinction is in its interludes, how should it be fitted for the stage, save by the excision of all but the love of hero and heroine? Yet one nameless writer was courageous enough to attempt the impossible, and there is hidden in the Harleian Collection of Manuscripts a poor, foolish play, entitled *The White Æthiopian*, still-born of Heliodorus. From the very dawn of the drama, the playwright sought his motive in novels, and while the masters of the craft were content to steal a hint and make a masterpiece, the journeymen, clinging too close to their model, produced nothing better than a series of dialogues. When Tom Heywood failed to convert *The Golden*

Ass into a respectable masque, our unknown writer could not hope to turn so inconsequent a piece as the *Æthiopica* into a consistent assemblage of acts and scenes. And his enterprise fared so ill that not even literary curiosity can prompt an admiration of *The White Æthiopian.* No ingenuity of construction, no dignity of phrase redeems the reckless essay from contempt. In describing Theagenes (among the "dramatis personæ") as a "gymnosophist," and giving him for companions two other "gymnosophists," the author reveals a solitary flash of unconscious humour. But this is insufficient to condone a prologue, four acts, and an epilogue, composed in rhymed couplets and interrupted by songs. The play, perchance, was written by some student of the University, at once to display his erudition and to win him a welcome at a tavern. By a wayward chance it survives, while oblivion snatches much that is ten times more worthy, but not even its antiquity is likely to procure for it the honour of print.

Still more remarkable is William Lisle's famous *Historie of Heliodorus.* "Amplified, augmented, and delivered paraphrastically in verse."* The earliest

* This is the full style and title of a later edition: The famous Historie of Heliodorus. Amplified, augmented and delivered paraphrastically in verse; by their Majesties most humble subject and servant, William Lisle. Whereunto is added divers testimonies of learned men concerning the Author. Together with a briefe summary of the whole History. London. Printed by John Dawson for Francis Eglesfield, and are to be sold at the signe of the Marigold in Pauls Churchyard. 1638.

edition is dated 1631, and the prefatory fragments are enough to prove that, had William Lisle elected to write in prose, his work would have had a fantastical interest. For though he displays a profound ignorance of verse, he handles prose with an elaborate curiosity. The testimonies wherewith he prefaces the translation are set forth in the most whimsical terms. Here, according to Lisle, is Melancthon's judgment upon Heliodorus: "His style is neat, not smelling, full of excellent variety, delivering counsailes, occasions, events and affections even to life." Still more high-sounding is his version of Dempster's eulogy: "Heliodorus, the Phœnix of Phœnicia: an elegant writer of chast Love, and in the contexture of this history a most elaborate Author." And thereupon Lisle, laying hands on this Phœnix of Phœnicia, turns him to ashes. He elected the rhymed couplet to represent the prose of Heliodorus, and he wrote it like a schoolboy:

Blacke-winged night flew to th' Antipodes
At sight of Morning Starre, and the Easterne seas
With-held the rising Beame, untill it guilt
The top of trees, and turrets highest built.

And so on for many a weary page. Nor was he content with this experiment: he must needs reflect upon his own language in a metrical preface. Thus his criticism opens:

About the tongues when divers with me wrangle,
And count our English but a mingle-mangle,
I tell them, all are such, and in conclusion
Will grow so more by curse of first confusion.

The familiar style, the outlandish words, the tripping metre, remind you (at a distance) of Charles Cotton, and no serious work was ever introduced by so flippant a fragment.

But with William Lisle, English was not yet bankrupt in character, and it was a later generation that mimicked in another tongue the trivialities of the *Æthiopica*. For at last Heliodorus fell into the hands of Nahum Tate and a Person of Quality. Now, with the advent of the Person of Quality the art of translation died a miserable death. When this cultured abstraction, ill-equipped for the task, took the Englishing of Latin and Greek as its hobby, colour and distinction had vanished from our prose. The stateliness of the Tudor style was replaced by a glib facility, with naught to recommend it save a pretension of good sense and simplicity. Not one of the "Various Hands," for instance, who with Dryden's connivance murdered Lucian, rose to a proper understanding of his author, and yet all would doubtless have agreed that the ancient translators were outrageous barbarians who understood not their art. Assuredly not one of them understood it after the pedant's own fashion, and he who demands a word for word translation had better betake himself to Dr. Giles. There are, however, several methods of rendering the symbols of one language by the symbols of another. It was Robert Browning's opinion that "a translation should be literal at every cost save that of absolute violence to our language"; and Robert

Browning's own achievement in the *Agamemnon* should be enough to refute the opinion. For in that version not only is violence continually done to our language, but there is scarce a page intelligible without the Greek. A literal translation generally resembles a photograph: seemingly true to its original, it is essentially and inherently false. A reckless importance is given to trivial details, and while the outline of the object is still recognisable, its beauty and character are offered a sacrifice to a mistaken theory of accuracy. Transplant a verb or a substantive from one language to another, and it may lose all savour and significance: changing its place in a sentence, it cannot but change its effect. To an ear trained in the loose-knit license of English, the austerer syntax of Greek may appear somewhat hard and constrained; but to render Heliodorus by a rigid phrase would be to misreprent his aim and his meaning. In fact, the most accomplished translators have treated their originals with the utmost freedom, assuring themselves of fidelity by far subtler methods than the paltry correspondence of balanced words. Not seldom the shortest cut to an accurate version is an elaborate detour; not seldom is it necessary to recede as far as possible from the original to ensure a harmonising or a corresponding effect. But such was not the fashion of Nahum Tate's time, and we are fortunate to-day in returning to a juster appreciation of the true masterpieces. To contrast a single page written by this particular Person of Quality, who chose Heliodorus for his own with a page of Underdowne's sounding prose, is to distinguish a living, characteristic style from an effete and faded manner.

And yet, a worse fate was in store for Heliodorus—the fate of neglect. He is not adventurous enough to satisfy the common taste for blood, he is not introspective that the analyst should desire him. He is but a romantic, born out of season, blowing the trumpet, throwing down the glove, bidding his heroes enter the lists to compete for the smiles and the hands of fair women. If his episodes are old-fashioned to-day, it is because they have been unconsciously stolen by an unbroken line of novelists. But as he is not appointed to be read in schools, as his insipid style dismays the amateur, he is not likely to recapture his popularity. No, his best hope of immortality lies in the version of Underdowne. For Underdowne, though he had but little Greek, understood the language of Romance, and if he did not translate his author, he replaced him, with a version no less rich in invention than ingenious in style.

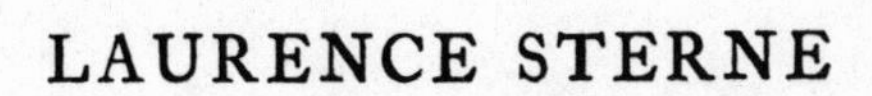

LAURENCE STERNE

LAURENCE STERNE

THE hero of primitive romance was the lusty picaroon, who wandered the world over in search of adventures. To help a damsel in distress or to cut a brother's purse—these were his simple-hearted ambitions. He knew no other motives than curiosity and an empty pocket; and as he was merry without reason, so he suffered without regret. Now and again his enterprises are tedious through lack of invention: so industriously does he pad the hoof along the familiar highway, so intimately does he accustom you to his prodigies, that his most marvellous escapes are seldom unexpected. But there is an enchantment even in his irresponsibility. For him murder and rapine are rather the expression of a joyous temper than the illustrations of a theory, he develops no character wherewith to flatter the psychologist, he runs his course from the cradle to the grave mainly for his own and his readers' disport, and he wins the world's gratitude in that, though he may lapse into dulness, his purpose is seldom the improvement of mankind.

Now the brain, too, has its adventures: there is a

picaresque, also, of the intellect. This other adventurer wanders in a limitless and ever-changing land, where the highroad is set with ideas for trees, where there are no flowers save sparkling epigrams. Here the only pockets picked are the brains of others, the maidens succoured are generous impulses; here, instead of lives taken, reputations are unlaced. And a very pretty fellow he may appear, this intellectual picaroon. He is akin to Lucian, to Athenacus, to Rabelais, to Burton. Never weary of exploring the waste-places of knowledge, he will break a lance with every passing paradox, and with the sword of satire in his hand will rescue Wit from the dungeon of Stupidity. No enterprise is too high for his courage, no desert too remote for his discovery, and you may set out with him when you will, confident that he will lead you through pleasant places, and will solace the journey with deeds of speculative intrepidity. To this ingenious confraternity Laurence Sterne belongs; and if *Gargantua* be the *Robinson Crusoe* of the intellect, if the *Anatomy* be the *Gulliver* of the brain, then *Tristram Shandy* takes its place in this assembly of gallant ventures as the *Gil Blas* of the spirit, separated always by a discreet distance from the peerless *Don Quixote de la Mancha*, the supreme example of the picaroon in mind and prowess whereof the world's literature may boast.

For Laurence Sterne is a prince among literary tramps, a king in the Bohemia of phrase and fable. He takes the road with a debonair frivolity, starting nowhere to go nowhither. He recognises no purpose in his travel, save his determination to be rid of useless encumbrance; it even irks him to keep to the big road, and no sooner has he ambled a dozen paces than he skips over a stile or takes a bridle-path. To follow his track is an enterprise impossible; as surely as you catch a glimpse of him trudging on ahead, so surely shall he elude you at the next corner. His *Tristram Shandy* is a triumph in the art of digression. Never was a book patched together (you cannot say composed) with so little sense of a plan or of a hero. Its very title, *The Life and Opinions of Tristram Shandy, Gent.*—is purposely misleading, since as Tristram is not born until the third volume, so we know little more of his career, save a misadventure with a window-sash, the dignity of his breeching, and his departure for the grand tour; while that critic would be a miracle of ingenuity who should disengage from the nine volumes a single opinion that does not belong rather to the author than to his puppet.

At the outset Sterne describes his policy, or rather lack of policy, with unwonted circumstance, and for the moment we are compelled to give him our allegiance. "Therefore, my dear friend and companion," he writes in the first volume, "if you should think me somewhat sparing of my narrative on my first setting out—bear with me,—and let me go on, and tell my story in my own way; or, if I should seem now and then to trifle upon the road,—or should sometimes put on a fool's cap with a bell to it, for a moment or two as we pass along—don't fly off,—but, rather, courteously give me credit for a little more wisdom than appears upon my outside;—and, as we jog on, either laugh with me or at me, or in short do anything,—only keep your temper." To keep your temper is seldom difficult, even if the artifice or digression, pushed beyond the limit of humour, robs you of your patience. But you hesitate before you give the author "credit for more wisdom than appears on the outside," since it is evident that when he set the full-stop to volume two, he knew not what volume three would bring forth. He designed the book for a medley of humour and reflection, of pathos and impertinence. He dreamed half seriously of Shandeism raised to a philosophy; his vanity almost prayed that a habit of life might proceed from the turns and twists of his flippancy. "I have converted many unto Shandeism," he wrote to Garrick from Paris—"for be it known, I Shandy it away fifty times more than ever I was wont, talk more nonsense than ever you heard me talk in your days—and to all sorts of people." No wonder the Comte de Choiseul was amazed. "Qui le diable est cet homme-là, ce Chevalier Shandy," he is said to have asked, thereby enchanting Sterne. And by an irony the Chevalier is remembered most tenderly as a delineator of character. To reflect upon his masterpiece is to call up the images of My Uncle Toby and My Father, of Yorick and Trim, of My Mother and Dr. Slop. The preference is just and inevitable. The personages of the book are more ingenious than its theory, but they chime with their author's aimlessness, and you will better appreciate them if first you master the principles of Shandeism.

Shandeism, then, is a genial humour tempered by an exaggerated sensibility. There are no facts nor fictions of life which may not be resolved in accordance with its tenets, if only it be remembered that the grave controversy must be flippantly considered, that a proper solemnity puts the best face upon a frivolous discussion. Erudition, false by preference, is a necessary accompaniment, and the witty story a pleasurable interlude. The theory, as well as its exposition, is borrowed from Rabelais; and Sterne, ever a thrifty soul, is scarce original in his own defence. "True Shandeism," he says, with more than a reminiscence of Pantagruel, "think what you will against it, opens the heart and lungs, and, like all those affections which partake of its nature, it forces the blood and other vital fluids of the body to run freely through its channels, makes the wheel of life run long and cheerfully round."

A well-founded boast, so far as touches the humour of Shandeism. For Sterne is humorous not only in his character but in his incident. What could be wittier, for all its theft, than the various spirit wherein the news of My brother Bobby's death is received? Where is a scene conceived in a finer vein of folly than the bed of justice, held upon the Breeching of Tristram? The *Tristrapædia*, moreover, is a marvel of whimsical instruction. And the episode of the midwife, the clauses of My

Mother's marriage-settlement, the dissertation upon Christian names, the influence of nose upon character, Mr. Shandy's incomparable letter concerning love and its dietary—are not these separate oddities treated with a learning that is ever gay, with a gaiety that is ever learned? But before all is the habit of disputation most pompously burlesqued, and a climax is reached when the decay of eloquence is gravely ascribed with a true Rabelaisian touch to "nothing else in the world but short coats and the disuse of trunk hose." Nor is the wayward design of the chapters one whit less amusing: it is impossible, for example, to withhold a laugh from the King of Bohemia, whose story never gets told by Corporal Trim. And none ever compassed, *πυρὰ προσδοκίαν*, more or more delightful topsy-turvydoms of speech: "We'll go, brother *Toby*, said my father, whilst dinner is coddling—to the Abbey of Saint Germain, if it be only to see these bodies, of which Monsieur *Sequier* has given such a recommendation.—I'll go see anybody, quoth my uncle *Toby;* for he was all compliance through every step of the journey.—Defend me! said my father—they are all mummies.—Then one need not shave, quoth my uncle *Toby*." The irrelevance of that reply is a joy which no familiarity can stale.

But if Sterne tickled the humours of incongruity with the lightest of light fingers, if he made a wise man's sport with the follies of erudition, he failed, as only a sentimentalist can fail, in the province of pathos. Once he changes laughter for tears, he loses all sense of proportion. There is no trifle, animate or inanimate, he will not bewail, if he be but in the mood; nor does it shame him to dangle before the public gaze those poor shreds of sensibility he calls his feelings. Though he seldom deceives the reader into sympathy, none will turn from his choicest agony without a thrill of æsthetic disgust. The *Sentimental Journey*, despite its interludes of tacit humour and excellent narrative, is the last extravagance of irrelevant grief. The road from Calais to Paris is watered with Yorick's tears. Whether a dead ass or a live starling be the excuse, whether the misery spring from the absent Eliza or the very present Maria, the pose and folly of the mourner are not dissembled. Though it were easy to prove that Sterne was stoically indifferent to the woes of others, the demonstration is inapposite, since a writer may be a monster of cruelty and yet possess the talent of moving his readers to a willing grief. But genuine sentiment was as strange to Sterne the writer as to Sterne the man; and he conjures up no tragic figure that is not stuffed with sawdust and tricked out in the rags of the green-room.

Fortunately, there is scant opportunity for idle tears in *Tristram Shandy*, whose spirit of burlesque is too volatile for pathos. Yet no occasion is lost, and the joyous comedy is not without its blemishes. Yorick's death is false alike to nature and to art. The vapid emotion is properly matched with a commonness of expression, and the bad taste is none the more readily excused by the suggestion of self-defence. Even the humour of My Uncle Toby is something degraded by the oft-quoted platitude: "Go, poor devil," says he, to an over-grown fly which had buzzed about his nose, "get thee gone. Why should I hurt thee? This world surely is big enough to hold both thee and me." And who would not spare Le Fevre's lachrymose death-bed at the inn? Sentimentality, indeed, is Sterne's sorriest weakness, and if it makes but a modest encroachment upon *Tristram Shandy*, it turns many of the *Letters* to ridicule, and reserves its worst excesses for that journey of reflection, "through France and Italy," where the mind wanders further afield than the body, where the true traveller is the brain.

But though *Tristram* is free from the grosser taint of pathos, it is marred by a kindred vice. In places it is manifestly obscene. Now, in life, obscenity may prove immoral; in literature, it is a question of taste; and it is improper, as well as superfluous, to charge Sterne with an outrage upon the virtues. The Puritan, through lack of imagination, is wont to try literature by the same narrow standard which strengthens him to condemn the conduct of his brothers. He no sooner reads of an impropriety, than he visualises it, and, bereft of humour, shudders at what he deems the wickedness of print. As though an artist were guilty of every act he chronicles! As though every jest, transcending the experience of the suburbs, should be brought to justice and visited with the common fine of forty shillings! But Sterne's offence being proven, acquittal is impossible despite the extenuating circumstances. He is not overtly immoral, alas! he is only too pure. He is always hankering after a licence he dare not enjoy; and his obscenity is but his sentiment in another form. Each vice springs from a constant incapacity to see things in a sane relation. Had Sterne always been as frank as Rabelais, you had not noticed the indecency. Also, that he could be frank, if he pleased, there are a dozen passages to prove. My Uncle Toby's courtship is without reproach, since the Widow Wadman never encountered her bashful lover without a boisterous rally. And the invention of the earlier chapters is as fresh as their treatment is sound.

But while Rabelais' laugh, open and rotund, is borne upon the ear without shame and without disguise, Sterne too often sniggers and smirks at his reader's surprise, proving that, whether he be sentimental or obscene, he is still self-conscious. As he poses for a marvel of sensibility, so he would appear completely emancipated. "Behold," he cries, "how valiantly I tread the orderly conventions beneath my feet! Am I not, as Voltaire would have it, the English Rabelais? Is there any ordinance of purity which I respect!" And the answer comes: "Yes, you respect them all; you are the legitimate ancestor of the impuritans, who have made our own generation an occasion of ridicule. When you would be brave, you are tiresome. You attempt, with the satisfaction of the salacious schoolboy, to tickle the sensibility of the innocent. But you never cease to exclaim upon your freedom, to boast of your jollity in that spirit of self-consciousness which convicts you of a malicious and inartistic purpose. In brief, you omit no opportunity of blinking behind the arras, and your indecency proceeds not from what you reveal, but from what you cover up, with your ogling shamefacedness." Between Yorick and Rabelais lies the chasm impassable. "Never trust those men," said Pantagruel, "that always peep out at one hole." And Sterne is among the untrustworthy. Whatever be the topic, he will, an he can, pervert it to an unuttered obscenity. He has not even the excuse of delighting in strange words. An unwonted expression, a forbidden word, lights up a page, as the friends of Gargantua know, with irresistible effect. There is none fit to appreciate good literature that applies the full-blooded, wanton joyousness of Rabelais or Petronius to the experience of common life. Colour, movement, unexpectedness, are the qualities of a humour that is broad as well as wholesome, and these qualities appeal to the literary sense alone.

But Sterne is ever reticent; he is always "macerating his sensuality." Only on one page of his book does he use conspicuously "bad" words, and then he divides them between an abbess and a novice. Nor does his attempted justification palliate his impure purity. "Heaven is witness," he protests, "how the world has revenged itself upon me for leaving so many openings to equivocal strictures—and for depending so much as I have done, all along, upon the cleanliness of my reader's imagination." 'Tis said, of course, in irony, since he always insists that his "reader's imagination" should supply the words his own tongue dare not utter. Aposiopesis is the essence of *Tristram*, as it is the end of the *Sentimental Journey*, and there is an artistic meanness in setting an ox upon your tongue, and reproaching those you invite to drive it off. "Heaven forbid," he wrote again in a famous letter, "the stock of chastity should be lessened by *The Life and Opinions of Tristram Shandy*," and, as only the dullard or the maniac deadens or enhances his chastity by literature, the prayer was doubtless heard. But there is an artistic as well as a moral chastity, "by nature, the gentlest of all affections;" and Sterne "gave it its head," so that with him "'tis like a ramping and a roaring lion."

Frankness, in brief, is the only purity; and while Rabelais is without blame, the reticence of Sterne too nearly resembles a purposed sentimentality, the inhuman horror of the modern novel. And all the while he hoped his "indecorums" might prove a source of profit. He confides to Garrick an ingenious arrangement made with Crébillon: each should recriminate upon the "liberties" of the other, and the money should be divided equally. Though the pamphlet never appeared, it was "good Swiss-Policy," but not the artifice of a writer affronted by "unclean imaginations." Worse still, the "obscenity" is commonly dull. The mind which delights in the Abbess of

Andouïllets, and laughs over the embarrassment of Phutatorius with the chestnuts, will honestly deplore the dead ass, and believe that the Traveller's tears welled from an honest and a sympathetic heart.

When we turn from Shandeism to the characters of the romance, there is naught but praise for the author. It is of a piece with Sterne's whimsicality, that setting out upon a voyage of reflection, he was happiest with the personages he encountered by the way. To speak temperately of the brothers Shandy is impossible, and were ungracious. They are eternal with the eternity of literature. From the mist of false erudition and flippant Shandeism they emerge, poignantly realised and exquisitely shaped. How could either find a better foil? My Father's habit of contention is most admirably countered by My Uncle Toby's *Argumentum Fistulatorium;* the complex folly of the one could not be more nicely balanced than by the childlike gravity of the other. The innocence of My Uncle Toby does but increase his humanity, and none that is his friend endures him off his hobby-horse. Whenever My Father's erudition is befogged by My Uncle Toby's simplicity, laughter is inevitable, and the persistence wherewith Uncle Toby accepts Mr. Shandy's metaphysical discoveries as contributions to the art of fortification is never tedious. And Sterne was vividly conscious of the excellence of his own creation. "So much am I delighted with My Uncle Toby's imaginary character," he wrote to Lady ——, "that I am become an enthusiast," and the world is easily persuaded to share his enthusiasm. One knows not which is the more admirable, the Captain's hobby-horse or the Captain's courtship, while Trim, with his Montero hat and his Turkish tobacco pipes, is the properest and most fantastical of corporals.

More complicated, yet in a sense less original, is My Father's personality—more complicated, because it depends upon the quips and cranks of sham learning—less original, because it is drawn from books as well as from life. From one point of view it is a literary concretion. Mr. Traill, in his excellent monograph, would have him a personification of "theory run mad," but whether such be the intent, or whether he be an anthropomorphism of Burton's *Anatomy*, he is still the most whimsical philosopher in literature. And My Mother—with what skill is her unyielding stupidity suggested! Despite her few appearances, she and her invincible irresponsiveness are as familiar as Mr. Shandy's antic knowledge or My Uncle Toby's amiability. And the others—Dr. Slop, the man-midwife, the honest, sensitive Corporal, the alluring Widow Wadman, even Susanna and Bridget—are they not all drawn with as sure a hand as the Shandy brothers, if with less distinction than that noble pair?

This briefly is the unrivalled achievement of the book: to have furnished forth a gallery of living portraits, whose features the world is as likely to forget as to despise. And the characters live, because Sterne never disdained nature. Had his father not been captain in a marching regiment, My Uncle Toby and the Corporal might have lacked verisimilitude. Even when he coloured his observation with caricature, he still drew from life, and his less amiable personages were recognised with resentment. Dr. Slop was known at once for a travesty of Dr. Burton, a Jacobite, whom Sterne's uncle had arrested upon a charge of high treason. And a certain nameless doctor attacked the author of *Tristram* in set terms for having, as he said, dishonoured the memory of Dr. Mead. The controversy matters not a jot to-day, and is only memorable because it illustrates Sterne's theory of portraiture, and gave him an opportunity to justify his work, as well as to prove how fallacious is the maxim "de mortuis nil nisi bonum."

But not only had he met his characters in the flesh; many a picturesque episode, many a dramatic scene, was prompted by his long experience of a Yorkshire village. Shandy Hall, its intimates and estates, had an existence, you are sure, in the neighbourhood of Stillington. To quote a single instance: when My Aunt Dinah left My Father a legacy of a thousand pounds, he straightway debated whether he should enclose Oxmoor, "a fine, large, whinny, undrained, unimproved common," or send My Brother Bobby forth upon the Grand Tour. Similar projects of enclosure engrossed the country clergyman, and thus he complains to his cousin: "'Tis a church militant week with me, full of marches and counter-marches—and treaties about Stillington Common, which we are going to enclose." Such then is the relation of the romance to life, and such the faculty of observation whereby it is separated from its distinguished model, *The Anatomy of Melancholy*.

But if Sterne owed much to experience, he owed more to books, and it is impossible to consider *Tristram Shandy* apart from its origins. Yet so consummately shameless are the thefts of Yorick, that reproach is forgotten in amazement. Like a true highwayman, he commits his robberies on every road of literature. Without hesitation or remorse, he bids his betters stand and deliver, tricking out his own person with whatever treasures fall into his hand. His debt to Rabelais was patent from the first; indeed he never ventured upon concealment. The very framework of his book is borrowed, and for Shandean read Pantagruelian, and you recognise that not even the philosophy is original. Careless as he commonly is of expression, he does not disdain to prig the cadence of a phrase. "Now, my dear anti-Shandeans, and thrice able criticks and fellow-labourers (for to you I write this Preface)"; thus Sterne echoes the first lines of Urquhart's *Gargantua*: "Most noble and illustrious drinkers, and you thrice precious pockified blades (for to you and none else do I dedicate my writings)."

But it was not until the appearance of Dr. Ferriar's *Illustrations* that the full measure was taken of Yorick's depredation. Never was a stranger tribute paid by disciple to his master. It was for Sterne's sake, said Ferriar, that he plodded through "miry ways of antic wit, and quibbling mazes drear;" as well might a prosecuting counsel claim the gratitude of the prisoner skulking in the dock. For this disciple convicted his master of indiscriminate and unwarrantable theft. It is true that once upon the quest he pushes his ingenuity too far, and makes discoveries which the finest subtlety might overlook. But the main charge is most ably sustained, and *Tristram* is revealed, in one aspect, an industrious mosaic. Rabelais and Beroalde, Montaigne and Bishop Hall, Bruscambille and Burton are one and all laid under contribution. Rabelais' part in the chapter on Noses is indirectly acknowledged, and if, when Yorick relates the contest between Tripet and Gymnast, he omits to explain that it is taken from Urquhart's *Rabelais*, at least the fragment is printed between inverted commas. Moreover, his admiration for Pantagruel is plainly avowed. "By the ashes of my dear Rabelais, and dearer Cervantes" is the choicest of his oaths, and more than once he quotes openly from the curate of Meudon.

But his respect for Burton is at once more secret and more practical. Though he nowhere mentions his master's name, he lies under a hundred unrevealed obligations. Not only does he adapt the habit of erudite quotation, but he steals quotation, phrase, and all. For instance, Mr. Sterne's edifying reflections upon the death of My Brother Bobby are lifted bodily from the *Anatomy*. One example of his method will serve as well as another, but surely parallel columns never exposed a more abandoned conveyance:

Sterne.	Burton.
Returning out of Asia, when I sailed from Ægina towards Megara, I began to view the country round about. Ægina was behind me, Megara was before me, Pyræus on the right hand, Corinth on the left. What flourishing towns now prostrate on the earth! Alas! alas! said I to myself, that a man should disturb his soul for the loss of a child, when so much as this lies awfully buried in his presence. Remember, said I to myself again—remember that thou art a man.	Returning out of Asia, when I sailed from Ægina towards Megara, I began to view the country round about. Ægina was behind me, Megara before, Pyræus on the right hand, Corinth on the left; what flourishing towns heretofore now prostrate and overwhelmed before mine eyes! Alas, why are we men so much disquieted with the departure of a friend, whose life is much shorter, when so many goodly cities lie buried before us? Remember, O Servius, thou art a man; and with that I was much confirmed, and corrected myself.

True, Sterne confesses the passage an extract from Servius Sulpicius' consolatory letter to Tully; true also, with characteristic whimsicality, he makes My

Uncle Toby, mindful of My Father's concern in the Turkey trade, put the question: "And pray, brother, what year of our Lord was this?" But there is no mention of Burton, and Sterne maybe trusted with whole-hearted confidence to the ignorance of his fellows. Meaner still are the paltrier loans—the loans of phrase or witty turn. Even if it be pleaded that a tangle of quotations comes apt to the purpose of *Tristram*, the pilfering of a line has no justification. Yet Sterne, having gone once to the cupboard, cannot stay his hand. "But where am I?" he exclaims, involved in too deep a consideration; "and into what a delicious riot of things am I rushing?" A travesty, in fact, of one of Burton's conclusions: "But where am I? into what subject have I rushed?" Again, cries Sterne in his preface: "Lay hold of me—I am giddy—I am stoneblind—I'm dying —I am gone—Help! help! help!"; and again Dr. Ferriar quotes from Burton: "But, hoo! I am now gone quite out of sight: I am almost giddy with roving about."

But in his eagerness to keep up an appearance of honesty, Sterne permits himself a still more daring freedom: he steals Burton's own condemnation of the plagiarist. "Shall we for ever make new books as apothecaries make new mixtures," asks this stalwart champion of originality, "by pouring only out of one vessel into another? Are we for ever to be twisting and untwisting the same rope, for ever in the same track, for ever at the same pace?" And turning to

Burton you trace the ironical felony: "As apothecaries we make new mixtures every day, pour out of one vessel into another; and as those old Romans robbed all the cities of the world, to set out their bad-sited Rome, we skim off the cream of other men's wits, pick the choice flowers of their tilled gardens, to set out our own sterile plots. . . . . We weave the same web still, twist the same rope again and again." How Sterne must have laughed at his own impudence! Yet the criminal cannot escape with a laugh, and he leaves the inquiry with many a stain upon his character.

In truth, he oversets all one's theories of plagiary. When Virgil was charged with stealing from Ennius, he answered, without a thought of his victim: "I did but take pearls from a dung-heap." Neither Shakespeare nor Molière, one fancies, felt an acute sympathy with the writers they plundered; and they are readily absolved, since the greatest can do no wrong. They stripped their inferiors, that is all; and rewarded them with a vicarious immortality. But Sterne picked the brains of wiser men. Yorick's most ardent admirer would scarcely insist that Burton and Rabelais were honoured by the contribution levied upon them. No: he tricked himself out in the plumage of nobler birds, and claimed the stolen feathers for his own. Even his sermons profited by his thievery, and those there are who decree this his most heinous sin. But the question is over subtle, and the flippant may urge that the sacred occasion gave but a pleasant sauce to his humour. Tried by the easiest code of morals, he is found guilty, since there is no law of literary honour that he does not violate. Yet his very flippancy saves him from a heavy sentence, especially as he may plead in extenuation an absence of motive.

However much of its satire *Tristram* owes to Burton's erudite collections, Sterne did not lack wit, and he might have composed his book without incurring a single debt. Was he then guilty of a vulgar kleptomania? Was he unable to withhold his hand from the property of others? Or shall we set his villainy down to the humours of Shandeism? "Je prends mon bien où je le trouve," he might have murmured with a shrug of frivolity, esteeming his furtive villainy no worse than a culmination of his own philosophy. Yet another explanation is possible. He may have set a wanton trap to catch his readers. He may have planned a deliberate attack upon their ignorance. You like to believe it, and the belief does no injustice to his character. But whatever the excuse, his crime was successful. For a while he escaped detection with marvellous felicity, and so skilfully did he throw dust in the critics' eyes, that Diderot sets it down to his peculiar glory, that alone of his countrymen he was guiltless of theft. And when at last his robbery was revealed, the veil was lifted with so gentle a hand, that Yorick's wandering spirit could scarce resent the discovery. After all, let us temper the wind of justice to the shorn lamb of his iniquity, since that which is best in Sterne is still Sterne's own, and not all the pedants in the world could have improved by a touch the portrait of My Uncle Toby.

His style, on the other hand, is unborrowed, and, if at times it be admirably suited to the matter, it is seldom distinguished and uniformly inaccurate. He set out upon the road of authorship with a false ideal: "Writing," said he, "when properly managed, is but a different name for conversation." It would be juster to assert that writing is never properly managed, unless it be removed from conversation as far as possible. But familiarity is Sterne's essential weakness. He spins his sentences with a sublime nonchalance. The grammar may be topsy-turvy, the relatives in admired disorder; but he cares not, so long as he arrives at some sort of an effect. Words, as the materials of an art, have no fascination for him. His vocabulary, in fact, is scanty and impersonal; his construction is as loose and ill-strung as carelessness can make it. Seldom do you feel the words in a sentence held together by a firm and supple thread, and an indifferent passage is apt to astonish you by its dignity.

"He stood like Hamlet's ghost, motionless and speechless, for a full minute and a half, at the parlour door (Obadiah still holding his hand), with all the majesty of mud." Thus is Dr. Slop's entry described, and, though it is scarce a masterpiece, it is projected at once from the surrounding sobriety. Nor is this lack of distinction astonishing: Sterne's sentences suffer from the prevailing theory of the book. What digression is to a chapter, that parenthesis is to a period, and never, until you have accounted for many an intervening clause, may you arrive safely at an expected conclusion. But if Sterne was not accomplished in the use of words and the facture of sentences, if he found grammar a perpetual difficulty and substituted a confusion of dashes for a reasoned punctuation, he had a brilliant gift of dramatic presentation—one chief element of style—and could set forth an argument or realise a scene with uncommon vividness. No artist in words, he was still a master of the picturesque, always true to his own ideal, that writing and conversation were one and the same art.

His influence was immediate and only too far-reaching. Nor did this expert in robbery view the sins of others with a lenient eye. "I wish from my soul," said he, "that every imitator in Great Britain, France, and Ireland had the farcy for his pains." Most shameless were those who anticipated by spurious travesties the later volumes of *Tristram*. There was John Carr, for instance, honourably famous for his translation of Lucian, who printed a third volume in 1769, and asked the world to believe that it was from the hand of the master. For thirty years similar deceits were practised with a similar ineptitude. No sooner was Yorick dead than *The Posthumous Work of a Late Celebrated Genius, deceased* (1770) astonished the town. The parody was sorry enough, yet it was presently reissued with its title changed to *The Koran*, was turned into French, and was at last fastened upon one Richard Griffiths, the son or husband of a popular novelist. Then there were the endless travels wherewith the incompetent attempted to steal a rag of reputation, such as *Yorick's Sentimental Journey Continued* (1793). Nor must the cloud of pamphlets be forgotten. As early as the May of 1760 there was published *The Clockmaker's Outcry against the Author of Tristram Shandy*, which drew from Sterne the wish "that they would write a hundred such," though he naturally resented the impertinence of those who attributed to himself a scurrilous epistle, *To my Cousin Shandy on his Coming to Town.*

In France, as in England, Shandeism had its followers, and *La Quinzaine Angloise* (1777), which purported to be a translation from the English, is a singularly ingenuous account of a pigeon and his rook. But the least contemptible of a poor lot is Gorgy, whose name was intended for an anagram of Yorick, and whose imitation was open and avowed. He, too, kept up the fiction of a posthumous work and described his *Nouveau Voyage Sentimental* as "the translation of a few sheets of manuscripts which served to cover some merchandise from London." If the machinery and style are Sterne's, the dulness is all the unknown author's own. Flat and tepid, it lacks the point and humour of the original. But Yorick's artifice is most faithfully reproduced. Here is the chapter without a heading; there is the deferred preface. The tears shed would float a ship, and while La Fleur is amplified to stupidity, a chapter is added upon the ways and habits of the *grisette*. This came in 1785, and six years later were printed *Les Tablettes sentimentales du bon Pamphile*, memorable only for the conversion of My Uncle Toby into M. de Bosstacq, who resembles his original in a lame leg and a hobby for fortification. Shandean also was *Ann'quin Bredouille*, a series of six tiny pamphlets, half an imitation of Sterne, half a commentary on the Revolution. It seems fatuous enough to-day, nor will the blank page, "cadre à remplir par le lecteur," and Yorick's other tricks endear it to the reader. "C'est tout bonnement," writes Gorgy, "un petit cousin de Tristram Shandy, un peu allié aux Rabelais, aux Merlin Cocaye, aux Scarron, et pour le prouver aux incredules, ce sera par defunte Jacqueline Lycurgues, actuellement Fiffre Major au Greffe des menus Derviches." There is naught else to say save that the work is well-nigh inaccessible, and that none will regret its rarity.

A far better echo is *Jacques le Fataliste* (1796), but even Jacques, despite his ingenuity, is not hilarious. Not only does Diderot honestly confess the source of his inspiration ; he descends in places to faithful adaptation. The relation of master to servant is freely borrowed from My Uncle and the Corporal, while in such passages as the dissertation upon names, and the love-making between Denise and Jacques, Sterne is almost literally reproduced. In a less degree you may trace Yorick's influence in that vivacious compost of obscenity and adventure, *le Compère Matthieu où les Bigarrures de l'esprit humain*, a piece of fantasy once attributed to Voltaire, but actually the work of the Abbé Dulaurens, who endured a thousand persecutions, and died a captive in 1797. In England Yorick's most conspicuous pupil was Henry Mackenzie, whose *Man of Feeling* is a sort of Shandy stripped of humour, and clothed with a pathos not anticipated in the most dolorous page of *The Sentimental Journey*. But more remarkable is Sterne's indirect influence. For all his dependence upon others, he added a new element to literature, and thus once more appears constant to the whim of contradiction. Since his death, there has not been published a single work of reflection or fancy but is subject to his example. And if he be not as widely read as Defoe or Swift, his style and theory have passed into the blood and substance of English literature.

His life, as we read it to-day, bears a strange likeness to his book. It is diversified by few incidents, nor ever disturbed by an adventure. A journey to London, a trip to the Continent, a fatally mild flirtation—these are its liveliest passages. Such facts as we know are best told by Sterne himself, for he is one of the few who have escaped the impertinence of casual biography. If the few memorials he left for his daughter's curiosity and a confused collection of letters are all that remain for the world's enlightenment, they provide as much as the world has a right to know. By his own account, then, Laurence Sterne was born at Clonmel on November 24, 1713; the son of a gallant officer, Roger Sterne, and of a widow, Agnes Nuttle, whose father-in-law was "a noted sutler in Flanders, in

Queen Ann's wars, where my father married his wife's daughter (*N.B.*—he was in debt to him)." His early years were spent in the tiresome wanderings demanded by the Captain's duty, though, to be sure, the family never lacked the excitements of births or deaths. Two incidents lend a glamour to his youth. "It was in this parish (of Animo)," thus he tells the story, "during our stay, that I had that wonderful escape in falling through a mill-race whilst the mill was going, and of being taken up unhurt. The story is incredible, but known for truth in all that part of Ireland—where hundreds of the common people flocked to see me." The miraculous escape recalls an experience of the infant Horace, and surely Yorick was not born to be drowned. The other legend is less credible, and still more wisely prophetic. It is of the hero's school-days, and again his own words shall convey the anecdote: "The schoolmaster says he had had the ceiling of the schoolroom new white-washed—the ladder remained there. I one unlucky day mounted it, and wrote with a brush in large capital letters LAU. STERNE, for which the usher severely whipped me. My master was very much hurt at this, and said, before me, that never should this name be effaced, for I was a boy of genius, and he was sure I should come to preferment."

In due course he was sent by his cousin to the University of Cambridge, where he was admitted of Jesus College, July 6, 1733, under the tuition of Mr. Cannon. As in duty bound he sent his own

Tristram to the same distinguished college, and to pay it a further honour swore by St. Rhadegunda, the patron saint of this ancient foundation. In 1741 he married Miss Lumley, who secured his affection by murmuring, when his heart was almost broken: "My dear Laurey, I can never be yours, for I verily believe I have not long to live—but I have left you every shilling of my fortune." However, the lady recovered to spend many years in amiable estrangement, and it was through her interest that he added to Sutton the living of Stillington.

Now, it was not until 1760 that Laurence Sterne revealed his talent to the world. Had he died before that year he would have descended to the grave in respectable obscurity. Like Fielding, like Cervantes, like Sir Walter, he came into the full possession of his talent at an age whereat the most of men are happy in the contemplation of their master-pieces. Yet the twenty years of retirement were not fruitless, and when, at last,* the first two volumes of *Tristram Shandy* were given to the world, their author was straightway proclaimed a man of genius, and his visit to London was nothing less than a triumph. He

* Thus were the volumes of *Tristram* published:

Volumes 1 and 2.—York, 1759. Printed for and sold by John Hinxham, Bookseller in Stonegate. London, 1760.

Volumes 3 and 4.—London, 1761. Dodsley.

Volumes 5 and 6.—London, 1762. }
Volumes 7 and 8.—London, 1765. } Becket and de Hondt.
Volume 9. —London, 1767. }

fell into the life of the court as though he had never strayed a mile from Whitehall, and had scarce an acquaintance without a title. His table, he takes care to tell his friends, was littered with invitations; in fact he Shandied it with excellent effect. "Any man who has a name," said Dr. Johnson, "or who has the power of pleasing, will be very generally invited in London. The man Sterne, I am told, has had engagements for three months." There is a certain scorn in the utterance, though when Goldsmith objected, "And a very dull fellow," Johnson replied with a generous and characteristic "Why, no, sir."

Patronised by the court, admitted to the friendship of Lord Bathurst, Sterne welcomed his belated celebrity with enthusiasm. The letters written in the early days of his triumph are joyous with an almost childlike joyousness. He hears debates in the Commons; he attends the ceremonies of state; and withal believes himself a very fine and dashing personage. Nor was Yorick sent empty away. No sooner were the two volumes published than he received from Lord Falconbridge the curacy of Coxwold—"a sweet retirement in comparison of Sutton." On the other hand there were those who sneered and carped at his success, and Sterne was assailed so bitterly with charges of indecent personality, that he was driven perforce to a defence. At the outset he explains the reason of his authorship: "Why, truly," he writes to Mrs. F——, "I am tired of employing my brains for other people's advantage.

'Tis a foolish sacrifice I have made for some years to an ungrateful person." Here is a protest against his uncle, on behalf of whose Whiggery Sterne had already squandered his gifts. This is a mere skirmish, and not until he was goaded to anger by an impertinent Doctor, did he attempt to justify himself in all seriousness. "You will get a penny by your sins, and that's enough," sneered the Doctor, and Sterne, having honestly owned that he "proposed laying the world under contribution when he set pen to paper," proceeds to an analysis of his motives. He opens with an idle profession of benevolence. "I had other views," he writes, "the first of which was the hopes of doing the world good, by ridiculing what I thought deserving of it." The occasion, no doubt, condones his hypocrisy, but his other statement, that if the book "is writ against anything, 'tis writ against the spleen," is at once more honest and more reasonable. Presently he discloses his real purpose in the oft-quoted assertion: "I wrote not to be fed, but to be famous," and the first few months of London must have convinced him of success.

But far more grievous was the charge of blackmail, caught up in gossip and repeated to him by Garrick. Sterne, it was said, and tacitly acknowledged, received a purse from Warburton, and the ingenuity of malice instantly suggested that the prelate had thus bought off a disgraceful appearance as Tristram's tutor. The reply, dated "Thursday, 11 o'clock —Night," is indignant and conclusive. "'Twas for all the world," wrote Sterne to Garrick, "like a cut across my finger with a sharp penknife. I saw the blood—gave it a suck—wrapt it up—and thought no more about it. But there is more goes to the healing of a wound than this comes to," and Sterne proves the groundlessness of the accusation with dignity and emotion, though not without a touch of Yorick's sentimentality. Surely, with the world at loggerheads over his masterpiece, the victim might have been spared this added infamy? Still, he lived to be described by Warburton as an "irrevocable scoundrel," and for a man of sensibility, he was strangely insensitive to assaults made upon his virtue.

The opening of *Tristram Shandy* was followed by the appearance of Yorick's *Sermons*, and from the first Sterne regarded his novel as a spring-board from which his spiritual counsel might take a higher leap. Published by a country rector, the sermons would have had no success: as the compositions of the amiable Yorick they claimed an eager and an immediate attention. None was so keenly conscious of this profitable curiosity as their author. The third and fourth volumes, he assured Mr. Foley, would bring him a handsome sum. "Almost all the nobility of England honour me with their names," he added, "and 'tis thought it will be the largest and most splendid list which ever pranced before a book, since subscriptions came into fashion." Thus he prospered, always buoyant and always in difficulties. In 1762 he made his journey in France, and two years later wandered through Italy in search of health. The appearance and reception of his books furnished the one reasonable excitement of his life, until in 1768 there was published *The Sentimental Journey*, in some respects his most characteristic and most finished performance.

If his life resembled his book in its paucity of incident, the resemblance of sentiment is remarkable also. Both in its whimsicality and its pathos, *Tristram Shandy* is largely autobiographical. Sterne was resolute in the cultivation of incongruous experience. A country clergyman, he entertained a very poor regard for his profession. Continually he complains of the duties laid upon him by the Church, and if he delights in subscription-lists, he has a poor opinion of sermon-making. "'Tis my vile errantry, as Sancho says, and that is all that can be made of it." Yet his sermons are but essays in worldliness, and suggest the pulpit only in their framework. Even in the pulpit he could not resist a pleasantry, and one wonders what thought the congregation of the Ambassador's Chapel in Paris, when he chose Hezekiah and the Messengers for the subject of his discourse. But his masterpiece is the discourse on the Prodigal Son, which contains an exquisitely Shandean paraphrase of the ancient legend. The Prodigal, declares the preacher, "was cheated at Damascus by one of the best men in the world; . . . a whore of Babylon swallowed his best pearl and anointed the whole city with his Balm of Gilead; . . . the apes and peacocks which he had sent for from Tharsis lay dead upon his hands; the mummies had not been dead long enough, which had been brought him out of Egypt." Doubtless the village audience listened in bewilderment, and Sterne was the more encouraged to fresh experiments upon the stolidity of his flock.

Again, the sentiment of his life is no more real than the sentiment of his book; yet he was for ever shedding tears over the unattainable. If it was not Kitty it was Eliza, but whatever the name, there was the same excuse for pathos and nobility of soul. Thackeray, after his own fashion, scolded Sterne as an usher might scold a naughty schoolboy, soundly rating him for his errors,* but the condemnation is wholly lacking in humour, since Sterne was ever an inveterate philanderer, who felt as lightly as he expected others to feel. His sympathy for Eliza is as genuine as his sympathy for the dead ass. In not one of the letters is there a line of passion, and the lady's departure left him imperturbed. Nor can you believe, without impertinence, that her own eyes were dim with tears. "Were your husband in England," wrote Sterne in what were supposed the throes of an illicit love, "I would freely give him five hundred pounds to let you sit by me two hours a day." And why this generous, this

* The climax of impertinent reproof is reached by the American Allibone, who thus sums up Sterne's villainy: "A standing reproach to the profession which he disgraced, grovelling in his tastes, indiscreet, if not licentious in his habits, he lived unhonoured, and died unlamented, save by those who found amusement in his wit or countenance in his immorality!"

impassioned offer? Because he is sure that *The Sentimental Journey* "would sell so much the better for it, that I should be reimbursed the sum more than seven times told." Is that the voice of guilty sentiment, which shocked the scruples of Mr. Thackeray? Is it possible that a critic with a sense of humour should grudge this elderly clergyman his diversion? True, if another had suggested that when Eliza's husband and his own wife were overtaken by death, a happier marriage might be made, censure would not have been unreasonable. But you need not give a malicious interpretation to a proposal, whose very extravagance commended itself to Sterne.

Thus he lived in an atmosphere of false and pleasing sentiment. And when death came upon him (in March 1768), it found him where he professed a hope to die—at a lodging. His thievery pursued him, even to his deathbed, since the prayer that he might breathe his last at an inn was stolen from Bishop Burnet. Truly no man of feeling ever so fantastically borrowed his sentiments! Dying in poverty, he was robbed of his sleeve links that the undertaker might be satisfied, and there is a dark and incredible story told on the authority of Malone, that, after his body had been laid in the burial-ground belonging to St. George's, Hanover Square, it was snatched and carried to Cambridge for dissection.

Still more strange is the circumstance of his tombstone. When Yorick died, Eugenius laid a marble slab upon his grave, "with no more than these three words of inscription, serving both for epitaph and elegy:

ALAS, POOR YORICK!

Yorick's creator was not thus fortunate. No stone marked the place, and when at last a monument was set up, they were strangers who paid the tardy homage. Their own excuse might have been invented by their idol. They proclaim themselves "brother masons," asserting that Sterne, "although he did not live to be a member of their society," always "acted by rule and square;" wherefore they "rejoice in this opportunity of perpetuating his high and irreproachable character to after ages." With that purpose, they inscribed upon the stone a dozen ill-made verses, and misled the "after ages" not only as to their "brother's" age, but as to the date of their "brother's" death. And the pious admirer does not complain: he merely reflects how gaily Sterne, that master of the incongruous, smiles in the Shades at this final triumph of incongruity.

APULEIUS

APULEIUS*

"THE Golden Ass" of Apuleius is, so to say, a beginning of modern literature. From this brilliant medley of reality and romance, of wit and pathos, of fantasy and observation, was born that new art, complex in thought, various in expression, which gives a semblance of frigidity to perfection itself. An indefatigable youthfulness is its distinction. As it was fresh when Adlington translated it "out of Latine" three centuries since, so it is familiar to-day, and is like to prove an influence to-morrow. Indeed, it is among the marvels of history that an alien of twenty-five—and Apuleius was no more when he wrote his *Metamorphoses*—should have revolutionised a language not his own, and bequeathed us a freedom which, a thousand times abused, has never since been taken away.

* "The XI Bookes of The Golden Asse, containing the Metamorphosie of Lucius Apuleius, interlaced with sundry pleasant and delectable Tales: with an excellent Narration of the Marriage of Cupid and Pysches, translated out of Latine into English, by William Adlington. 1566.

A barbarian born, a Greek by education, Apuleius only acquired the Latin tongue by painful effort. Now a foreigner, not prejudiced by an inveterate habit of speech, seldom escapes a curiosity of phrase. Where the language is the same, whether written or spoken, art is wont to lapse into nature. But there was no reason why Apuleius, who could not but be conscious of his diction, should ever deviate from artifice. His style, in truth, he put on as a garment, and it fitted the matter without a crease. His exotic vocabulary was the fruit of the widest research. He ransacked the ancient plays for long-forgotten words. He cared not where he picked up his neologisms, so they were dazzling and bizarre. Greece, his own Carthage, the byways of Rome, contribute to the wealth of his diction, for he knew naught of that pedantry which would cramp expression for authority's sake. The literary use of slang was almost his own invention. He would twist the vulgar words of every day into quaint, unheard-of meanings, nor did he ever deny shelter to those loafers and footpads of speech which inspire the grammarian with horror. On every page you encounter a proverb, a catchword, a literary allusion, a flagrant redundancy. One quality only was distasteful to him : the commonplace. He is ever the literary fop, conscious of his trappings and assured of a handsome effect.

In brief, he belonged to the African School, for which elaboration was the first and last law of taste. He may even have been a pupil of Fronto, the prime champion of the "elocutio novella", the rhetorician who condemned Cicero in that he was not scrupulous in his search for effect, and urged upon his pupils the use of "insperata atque inopinata verba." No wonder poor Adlington, whose equipment of Latin was of the lightest, hesitated for a while! No wonder that he complained that "the Author had written his work in so darke and high a stile, in so strange and absurd words, and in such new invented phrases as hee seemed rather to set it forth to shew his magnificencie of prose than to participate his doings to others!" But the difficulty is not invincible; and the adventurous have their reward. The prose sparkles with light and colour. Not a page but is rich inlaid with jewels of fantastic speech. For Apuleius realised centuries before Baudelaire that a vocabulary is a palette, and he employed his own with incomparable daring and extravagance.

Though his style be personal, the machinery of his story is frankly borrowed. The hero who, transformed by magic to an ass, recovers human shape by eating roses was no new invention. He had already supplied two writers with a motive; and the learned have not decided whether it was from Lucian (so-called) or from Lucius of Patrae that Apuleius got his inspiration.* But a comparison of the Latin version

* That the hero transformed to an ass was the motive of two Greek romances can hardly be doubted after Photius' statement. The one, he says, was the work of Lucius of Patrae (who wrote μεταμορφώσεών λόγους διαφόρους), the other the work of Lucian.

with its Greek forerunner, commonly attributed to Lucian, proves the debt a feather's weight. Whatever Apuleius conveyed, he so boldly changed and elaborated as to make the material his own. His method is a miracle of simplicity. He accepts the Λούκιος ἤ Ὄνος as a framework, sometimes following it word for word, yet decorating it with so lavish an array of phrases, tricking it out with episodes so fertile and ingenious, as to force you to forget the original in the copy. Only in a single incident does his fancy lag behind. His hero's interview with the serving-maid is chastened and curtailed. The professionally elaborate detail, wherewith Lucian enhances this famous episode, is touched by Apuleius with a light and summary hand. But elsewhere he appropriates to adorn. Though again and again the transference is verbal, the added ornament is entirely characteristic, and it is as unjust to charge the author with plagiarism as it were to

The Λούκιος ἤ Ὄνος, preserved in the works of Lucian, is doubtless one of the romances known to Photius. But its style and impartiality never for an instant suggest Lucian, who would have made the *Metamorphosis* a peg for satire. And modern scholars are for the most part agreed that Lucian was not the author. Other considerations prevent our assigning it to Lucius, who, it is said, ran to a greater length, while it would be difficult to set forth the story in briefer terms than are employed by the author of Λούκιος ἤ Ὄνος. Probably it is the work of neither, though it may well be the romance attributed to Lucius by Photius. The only sure fact is that in the Λούκιος ἤ Ὄνος are to be found the dry bones of *The Golden Ass*. The curious may consult Professor Rohde's *Ueber Lucian's Schrift* Λούκιος ἤ Ὄνος *und ihr Verhaeltniss zu Lucius von Patrae und den Metamorphosen des Apuleius.*

condemn the Greek tragedians for their treatment of familiar themes.

Indeed, the two writers approach the matter from opposite points of view. Lucian's austere concision is purely classical. He has a certain story to present, and he reaches the climax by the shortest possible route. The progress is interrupted neither by phrase nor interlude, and at the end you chiefly admire the cold elegance wherewith the misfortunes of Lucius are expressed, as it were, in their lowest terms. Apuleius, on the other hand, is unrestrainedly romantic. He cares not how he loiters by the way ; he is always ready to beguile his reader with a Milesian story—one of those quaint and witty interludes which have travelled the world over, and become part, not merely of every literature, but of every life. Our new fashion of analysis, our ineradicable modesty, have at last denied them literary expression, and to-day they eke out a beggarly and formless existence by the aid of oral tradition. But time was they were respectable as well as joyous. What reproach is attached to the widow of Ephesus, who has wandered from Petronius even unto Rabelais ? To what admirable purpose is the *Sermo Milesius* handled in the *Decamerone* to which Apuleius himself contributed one delectable tale ! Did not the genius of Balzac devise a monument proper to its honourable antiquity in the *Contes Drolatiques?* And yet the second century was its golden age, and none so generously enhanced its repute as Apuleius.

His masterpiece, in truth, is magnificently interlaced with jests, sometimes bound to the purpose of the story by the thinnest of thin threads, more often attached merely for their own or for ornament's sake. But not only thus is he separate from his model. Though he is romantic in style and temper alike—and romanticism is an affair of treatment rather than of material—he never loses touch with actuality. He wrote with an eye upon the realities of life. Observation was a force more potent with him than tradition. If his personages and incidents are wholly imaginary, he could still give them a living semblance by a touch of intimacy or a suggestion of familiar detail. Compare his characters to Lucian's, and measure the gulf between the two! Lucian's Abroea is a warning voice—that, and no more. Byrrhena, on the other hand, is a great lady, sketched, with a quick perception of her kind, centuries before literature concerned itself with the individual. And is not Milo the miser leagues nearer the possibility of life than Hipparchus? Even Palaestra, despite the ingenuity of one episode, is not for an instant comparable in charm and humour to Fotis, most complaisant of serving-maids.

Nor is it only in the portrayal of character that Apuleius proves his observation. There are many scenes whose truthful simplicity is evidence of experience. When Lucius, arrived in Hypata, goes to the market to buy him fish, he encounters an old fellow student—Pythias by name—already invested with the authority and insignia of an ædile. Now he, being a veritable jack-in-office, is enraged that Lucius has made so ill a bargain, and overturning his fish, bids his attendants stamp it under foot, so that the traveller loses supper and money too. The incident is neither apposite nor romantic; it is no more Milesian than mystical; but it bears the very pressure of life, and you feel that it was transferred straight from a note-book. Again, where will you find a franker piece of realism than the picture of the mill, whereto the luckless Ass was bound? Very ugly and evil-favoured were the men, covered only with ragged clouts; and how horrible a spectacle the horses, with their raw necks, their hollow flanks, their broken ribs!

The Greek author, disdaining atmosphere, is content to set out his incidents in a logical sequence. Apuleius has enveloped his world of marvels in a heavy air of witchery and romance. You wander with Lucius across the hills and through the dales of Thessaly. With all the delight of a fresh curiosity you approach its far-seen towns. You journey at midnight under the stars, listening in terror for the howling of the wolves or the stealthy ambush. At other whiles, you sit in robbers' cave and hear the ancient legends of Greece retold. The spring comes on and "the little birds chirp and sing their steven melodiously." Secret raids, ravished brides, valiant rescues, the gayest of intrigues—these are the diverse matters of this many-coloured book. The play of fancy, the variety of style, the fertility of resource are inexhaustible. Mythology is lifted into life, and life itself transformed to mystery at the wizard's touch. The misery and terror of the Ass's life are intercepted by the story of Cupid and Psyche, set forth with rare beauty and distinction of style. And yet this interlude, exquisitely planned and phrased, which suggested a worthless play* to Tom Heywood, and has been an inspiration to many poets, from Mrs. Tighe to Mr. Bridges, is the one conspicuous fault of the book. Admirable in itself, it is out of proportion as well as out of key; though you turn to it again for its own sake, you skip it industriously when it keeps you from robbery and witchcraft.

But the most remarkable characteristic of *The Golden Ass* is the ever-present element of sorcery, of the *Macabre*, as Mr. Pater calls it. Grim spectres and horrid ghosts stalk through its pages. The merriest Milesian jest turns sudden to the terror of death and corruption. The very story which Boccaccio borrowed is shifted by Apuleius to a weird conclusion. The baker, having most wittily avenged his wife's deceit, is lured into a chamber by a meagre, ragged, ill-favoured woman, her hair scattering upon her face, and when the servants burst open the door to find their master, behold! no woman, but only the baker hanging from a rafter dead! And where for pure horror will you match

* Loves Maistrese: or the Queen's Masque. As it was three times presented before their two EXCELLENT MAJESTIES, within the space of eight dayes. In the presence of sundry foraigne AMBASSADORS. 1636.

Meroe's mutilation of Socrates? Secretly the witch attacks him in his sleep, drives her sword deep into his neck, and dragging out his heart stops the wound with a sponge. Aristomenes, unwilling witness of the cruelty, half believes it a dream, and gladly they resume the journey, until, when Socrates goes to the river to drink, the sponge falls out and with it the last faint pulse of life. Again, when Thelyphron watches in the chamber of the dead lest witches should bite off morsels of the dead man's face, and falling asleep at sight of a weasel, loses his ears and nose, who so callous as to feel no shudder of alarm? But the most terrific apparition of all is the obscene priest of the Syrian goddess, with his filthy companions, carrying the divine image from village to village and clanging their cymbals to call the charitable. This grimy episode, with its sequent orgies, is related with an incomparably full humour which, despite its Oriental barbarity, is unmatched in literature.

So there is scarce a scene without its ghostly enchantment, its supernatural intervention. And herein you may detect the personal predilection of Apuleius. The infinite curiosity wherewith Lucius pries into witchcraft and sorcery was shared by his author. The hero transformed suffered his many and grievous buffetings because he always coveted an understanding of wizardry and spells; and Apuleius, in an age devoted to mysticism, was notorious for a magic-monger. Seriously it was debated, *teste* St. Augustine, whether Christ or he or Apollonius wrought the greatest marvels; and though the shape wherein the romance is cast induced a confusion of author and hero, it is recorded that Apuleius was a zealous magician, and doubtless it is himself, not Lucius, he pictures in his last book among the initiate. In the admirable description of Isis and her visitation, as of the ceremonies wherein he was admitted to the secret worship of the goddess, he departs entirely from his Greek original. Here, indeed, we have a fragment of autobiography. When in 158 A.D., at the dramatic moment of an adventurous career, Apuleius delivered his Apology—*pro se de magia*—before Claudius Maximus, he confessed that he had been initiated into all the sacred rites of Greece and had squandered the better part of a comfortable fortune in mysticism and the grand tour.

The main accusation was that he had won his wife—a respectable and wealthy widow—by magic arts. He was also charged with other acts of witchcraft and enchantment. Thattus, it was said, and a free-born woman had swooned in his presence, a piece of superstition which reminds you of Cotton Mather. But, replied Apuleius, with excellent humour and scepticism worthy of Reginald Scot, they were epileptics, who could stand in the presence of none save a magician. In brief, we cannot appreciate *The Golden Ass*, until we realise the modern spirit of curiosity which possessed its author. The lecturer's fame well-nigh outran the writer's. Apuleius travelled the length of civilised Africa with his orations, as the popular lecturer of to-day invades America ; and the majesty of Æsculapius, a favourite subject, was an excellent occasion for his familiar mysticism. He had been as intimately at home in the nineteenth century as in the second. Were he alive to-day, Paris would have been his field, and he the undisputed master of Decadence and Symbolism. The comparison is close at all points. Would he not have delighted in the Black Mass, as celebrated on the heights of Mont Parnasse? Like many among the makers of modern French literature he was an alien writing an alien tongue. His curiosity of diction, his unfailing loyalty to speech, his eager search after the strange and living word, his love for an art which knows no concealment—these qualities proclaim the Decadent. And that Symbolist is wayward indeed who finds not matter for his fancy in the countless stories which a perverse ingenuity has twisted a hundred times into allegory.

Such the author and his book. And when William Adlington, in the untried youth of English prose, undertook the translation of *The Golden Asse*, you would have thought no apter enterprise possible. Primitive and Decadent approach art in the same temper. Each is of necessity inclined to Euphuism and experiment. In the sixteenth century the slang, the proverb, the gutter phrase, which Apuleius brought back to the Latin tongue, were not yet sifted from English by the pedantry of scholars. But William Adlington, though an Elizabethan, was something of a purist. To be sure he was unable to purge his diction of colour and variety, and his manner was far better suited to the rendering of Apuleius than the prose of to-day, which has passed through the sieve of the eighteenth century. But with an excellent modesty he pleads acceptance for his "simple translation." Though he applauds the "franke and flourishing stile" of his author, "as he seems to have the Muses at his will to feed and maintaine his pen," he uses of deliberation "more common and familiar words"—the phrase proves the essential recognition of his own style—"fearing lest the book should appear very obscure and darke, and thereby consequently loathsome to the reader." Indeed he elected to translate the one book of the world which demanded the free employment of strange terms, and set himself incontinent to avoid slang and to simplify redundancies. And his restraint is the more unexpected when you recall the habit of contemporary translators. Barnaby Rich studded Herodotus thick with colloquialisms and fresh-minted words. Philemon Holland made no attempt to chasten his vocabulary. But Adlington, his opportunity being the higher, fell the more marvellously below it.

For the most part, then, you will ransack his version in vain for obsolete words or exotic flowers of speech. And yet not even his love of simplicity has kept his vocabulary entirely pure. Again and again a coined phrase, a strange form gleams upon his page like a dash of scarlet. "The rope-ripe boy" thus he renders "puer ille peremptor meus" by a happy inspiration, which

Apuleius himself might envy. Fresh and unhackneyed is "the gleed of the sun" for "jubaris orbe." How exquisitely does "a swathell of red silke" represent "russea fasceola": "traffe or baggage" is more pleasantly picturesque than "sarcinam vel laciniam," and one's heart rejoices to hear a churl styled "a rich chuffe." Again, "ungles" is far more expressive if less common than "claws"; and who would write "niggardly" when "niggish" is ready to his hand? And is not "a carraine stinke" a high-sounding version of "fetore nimio"? To encounter so sturdy and wholesome a phrase as "I smelling his crafty and subtil fetch"—though it be a poor echo of "ego perspiciens malum istum verberonem blaterantem et inconcinne causificantem"—is to regret the impoverishment of our English tongue. But not often are you rejoiced by the unexpected, and for the most part Adlington is a scrupulous critic of his diction.

As he makes no attempt to represent in English his author's vocabulary, so is he wont to shirk the imagery and curtail the redundancy affected by Apuleius, repressing the hyperbolical ostentations of his original, save only when he indulges in extravagances of his own. When the miserable Thelyphron is protecting a dead man from the witch woman thus does Apuleius, with his admirable sense of words, enhance the horror of crawling minutes: "cum ecce crepusculum et nox provecta et nox altior et dein concubia altiora; et jam nox intempesta" for which Adlington writes in all brevity "midnight." Apuleius again has a dozen fantastical notions of the dawn, and Adlington cuts them all down to the colourless level of "when morning was come." Thus even does he reduce so garishly purple a piece of imagery as, "commodum punicantibus phaleris Aurora roseum quatiens lacertum coelum inequitabat." When the thieves return to their den after the sack of Milo's house, and sit them down to revelry, Apuleius surpasses even his own habit of opulent description. "Estur ac potatur," thus he writes, "incondite pulmentis acervatim, panibus aggeratim, poculis agminatim ingestis." "Cups in battalions!" 'Tis a pretty conceit, and for Adlington it means no more than "they drank and eat exceedingly."

But having accustomed you to a chaste severity of language, he will break out suddenly into a decorative passage, for which the Latin gives no warrant. "Moreover there be divers that will cast off their partlets, collars, habiliments, fronts, cornets and krippins"; thus he turns a perfectly simple sentence—"lacinias omnes exuunt, amicula dimovent"—proving his quietude of phrase the effect of design rather than of necessity. So also he is wont to clip and crop his author's metaphors. "While I considered these things" is a withered, nerveless rendering of "cum isto cogitationis salo fluctuarem"; yet is it entirely characteristic of his method. Indeed, from beginning to end he treats his author with the freest hand, and never permits the form and colour of the Latin to interrupt his conception of English prose.

But if he sacrificed something by too scrupulous a

restraint, he sacrificed still more by his scanty knowledge of Latin. Scholarship was as little fashionable in Tudor England as pedantry, the defect corresponding to its quality; and Adlington laid no claim to profound erudition. He did but purpose, "according to his slender knowledge (though it were rudely, and farre disagreeing from the fine and excellent doings nowadayes)," to translate "the delectable jeasts of Lucius Apuleius into our vulgar tongue." Nor is the confession of "slender knowledge" a mere parade of modesty: it is wholly justified by the event. To compile a list of errors were superfluous. In truth, there is no page without its blunder, though, as we shall presently see, the translator commonly manages to tumble not only into sense but into distinction. Now and again the mistakes are so serious as to pervert the meaning, and then one regrets that Adlington was not more wisely guided. For instance, the servants of Philebus, the priest of the Syrian goddess, are called "puellae" by Apuleius in contempt of their miserable profession, and the translator impenetrably obscures the episode by rendering the word "daughters" without a hint of explanation.

Still, all are not so grave, though you are constantly driven to wonder at the ingenuity of error. When Byrrhena, in her panegyric of Hypata, tells Lucius that there the merchant may encounter the bustle of Rome, the quiet visitor enjoy the peace of a country-house, Adlington thus heroically misses the mark: "When the Roman-merchants arrive in this city they are gently and quietly entertained, and all that dwell within this province (when they purpose to solace and repose themselves) do come to this city!" Verily there is magnificence (of a kind) in such confusion; and how shall one reproach a translator, upon whom accuracy sets so light a burden? Again, with a sublime recklessness Adlington perverts "extorta dentibus ferarum trunca calvaria" into "the jaw-bones and teeth of wilde beasts," not pausing to consider the mere formality of grammatical concord. And when Fotis relates how Pamphile, having failed to advance her suit by other arts ("quod nihil etiam tunc in suos amores ceteris artibus promoveret"), designs to assume the shape and feathers of a bird, Adlington so carelessly confounds cause and effect as to say that the transformation was intended "to worke her sorceries on such as she loved."

"Tunc solus ignoras longe faciliores ad expugnandum domus esse majores?" asks one of the robbers; and Adlington, with the twisted cleverness of a fourth-form boy, extorts therefrom this platitude: "Why are you only ignorant that the greater the number is, the sooner they may rob and spoil the house?" When one of Psyche's wicked sisters threatens to go and hang herself if Psyche prove the mother of a god ("si divini puelli—quod absit—haec mater audierit, statim me laqueo nexili suspendam"), "if it be a divine babe," says the sister in the translation, "and fortune to come to the ears of the mother (as God forbid it should!) then I may go and hang my selfe:" thus ignorant was our Englishman of the commonest idiom. Once at the marriage of Charite, good fortune seemed to wait upon the Ass, and his mistress promised him hay enough for a Bactrian camel ("foenum camelo Bactrinae sufficiens"): a promise misinterpreted by a masterpiece of grotesquerie into "she would call me her little camell." With his very easy baggage of Latin, the translator lost the point of every catchword, and turned the literary allusion into nonsense. In the phrase "non cervam pro virgine sed hominem pro homine," the reference to Iphigenia is patent, and yet our excellent Adlington gets no nearer the truth than "not a servant for his maidens, but rather an Asse for himselfe!"

So much must be said in dispraise of what, after all, is a masterpiece of prose. The translator, said Dr. Johnson, "is to exhibit his author's thoughts in such a dress as the author would have given them had his language been English." Now, Adlington has failed, with the rest of the world, to reach this high standard. Under no conceivable circumstances could Apuleius have written in his terms and with his significance. For the perfect translation a knowledge of two languages is necessary. The modern translator is commonly endowed with a complete apprehension of Latin or Greek, and is withal lamentably ignorant of English. Adlington, on the other hand, was sadly to seek in Latin, but he more than atoned for his slender knowledge by an admirable treatment of his own language. Though he abandoned the colour and variety of Apuleius, he turned his author into admirable prose.

From the first page to the last you will not find a trace of foreign idiom. The result is not so much a fine translation as a noble original, fitted to endure by its vigorous diction and excellent rhythm. The manner is perfectly adapted to narration, and there are few can handle story with better delicacy and point. The style, if simple for its age, has all the distinction of simplicity. The cadences are a perpetual pleasure to the ear. There is a stateliness, a dignity of effect, which proves that the prose of the Authorised Version was no invention, but a growth.

Though Adlington does not pretend to echo the locutions of Apuleius, he is, after his own method, a master of phrase. "Girded with her beautiful skarfe of love"—is it not an exquisite idea? How more nearly or more adroitly would you turn "tamen nisi capillum distinxerit" than in these terms: "if her hair be not curiously set forth?" Did the modern translatord are to represent "ementita lassitudo" by "feigned and coloured weariness," there were hope that his craft might rise above journey-work. Who would complain that the original was embroidered when it is to such admirable purpose as: "Thus she cried and lamented, and after she had wearied herself with sorrow and blubbered her face with tears, she closed the windows of her hollow eyes, and laid her down to sleep." Here is prose, ever vivid and alert, ever absolved from the suspicion of the stereotyped phrase. In Adlington's day "good taste" had not banned freshness and eccentricity from the language.

A century later it had been impossible to translate "glebosa camporum" into "cloggy fallowed fields;" yet this is Adlington's expression, and it may be matched or bettered on every page.

Above all, his work is distinguished by that sustained nobility of rhythm which makes the Tudor prose the best of good reading. "And while I considered these things, I looked about, and behold I saw afarre off a shadowed valley adjoyning nigh unto a wood, where, amongst divers other hearbes and plesant verdures, me thought I saw divers flourishing Roses of bright damaske colour; and said within my beastiall mind, Verily that place is the place of Venus and the Graces, where secretly glistereth the royall hew, of so lively and delectable a floure:" here are no exotic words, no long-sought images; the rare effect is attained by a harmony which not even the sternest simplicity can impoverish. Or take a passage in another key: "In the meane season while I was fed with dainty morsels, I gathered together my flesh, my skin waxed soft, my haire began to shine, and was gallant on every part, but such faire and comely shape of my body was cause of my dishonour, for the Baker and Cooke marvelled to see me so slick and fine, considering I did eat no hay at all." Although the word "slick" (aptly suggested by "nitore") is, so to say, a high light, the beauty still depends upon the rhythm, to which Adlington's ear is ever attuned. In brief, whatever defects of scholarship and restraint mar the translation, it remains a model of that large, untrammelled prose which, before the triumph of common sense, seemed within the reach of all. But is it not the strangest paradox of literary history, that they who lived in the golden age of translation sought their original at second hand, or fumbled for their meaning in the dark!

One advantage at least was enjoyed by Adlington. He studied Apuleius in the native Latin, using, we may believe, the famous folio of 1500 (*cum Beroaldi commentariis*), prefaced by that *Vita Lucii Apuleii summatim relata*, which he paraphrased in English with his accustomed inaccuracy. Howbeit, he did not "so exactly pass through the author, as to point every sentence according as it is in Latine;" for so, he adds, "the French and Spanish translators have not done." Nor is there any doubt that he attempted to amend his ignorance of Latin by the aid of a French version. It is some proof of the early popularity of *The Golden Ass* that Spain, Italy and France had each its translation into the vulgar tongue before Adlington undertook the work. In 1522 there appeared a tiny quarto bearing this legend upon its title-page: "Lucius Apuleius de Lasne dore. . . . On les vend a Paris en la grand rue St. Jacques, Par Philippe le noir." It was by one Guillaume Michel; and though before the English translation was a-making there had appeared two other versions, the one by Georges de la Bouthiere (Lyons, 1553), adorned with cuts in the manner of Bernard Salmon, the other by I. Louveau d'Orleans, composed in 1553 and published at Lyons five years later, the earliest book was a guide, and too often a blind guide, unto Adlington's footsteps.

The Frenchman was the riper scholar, but not only did he indulge the tiresome habit of commenting by the way, and without warning, upon his text, but he was also guilty of the most ingenious blunders, which Adlington, as though his own errors were not sufficient, too readily followed. A comparison of the versions sets the matter beyond uncertainty. If again and again the same inaccuracy glares in English and French, it is obvious that the one was borrowed from the other. At the very outset there is a clear clue. Guillaume Michel, according to his habit of expansion, paraphrases "haec me suadente" in half a dozen lines ; Adlington, turning his invigilant eye from Latin, is guilty of the like unwarranted prolixity. Moreover, when Apuleius by a quip says of Meroe, "sic reapse nomen ejus tunc fabulis Socratis convenire sentiebam," you are puzzled by the ingenuity of Adlington's rendering : "being so named because she was a Taverner," until you turn to the French and find in "tavernière" the source of error.

Again, Diophanes, the magician in Milo's story, is consulted by a certain merchant, Cerdo by name. (The Latin is unmistakable : "Cerdo quidam nomine negotiator.") Now, Adlington boldly translates "a certaine Cobbler," and instantly the Frenchman's "quelque savatier" explains the blunder. "Toutfoys mon cheval et lautre beste lasne de Milo ne me voulurent souffrir avec eulx paistre:" so Michel at the beginning of the Fourth Book. And thus Adlington: "but myne own horse and Miloes Asse would not suffer me to feed there with them, but I must seeke my dinner in some other place." The renderings agree precisely in a gross inaccuracy, and the Latin "nec me cum asino vel equo meo compascuus coetus attinere potuit adhuc insolitum alioquin prandere foenum" is involved enough to explain Adlington's reliance upon the French. Another passage is even more convincing. "Ad quandam villam possessoris beati perveniunt," writes Apuleius, whom Adlington translates: "we fortuned to come to one Britunis house;" nor would it appear who this Britunis might be, unless you turned to Michel's French and read, "en aucun village chiez ung riche laboureur nomme Brulinus." This strange correspondence in error might be enforced by countless examples. But by this it is evident that, although Adlington did not, like Angell Day, Sir Thomas North, George Nichols (translator of Thucydides), render his author from the French openly and without shame, he consulted the French as well as the Latin, and fared rather the worse therefor.

If for a judgment of Adlington the writer there is ample material, of Adlington the man we know nothing more than he vouchsafes himself. That six editions appeared in some seventy years is proof of the book's popularity. But its only mention is in the Register of the Stationers' Company, where it figures "In the enterynge of Coopyes" between July 22, 1565, and July 22, 1566, something earlier than the date of the dedication. "Wekes. Recevyd of henry wekes," thus it runs, "for his lycense for pryntinge of a boke intituled *the hole boke of lucious apelious of ye golden asse*, viijd." The epistle dedicatory to Thomas, Earl of Sussex, is dated "from University College in Oxenford, the xviii. of September 1566."* But whether or no he was a graduate of that seat of learning is still uncertain. His name does not appear in the Register of the University, and in vain you consult the common sources of information. He presents his book to his patron in the customary terms of extravagant eulogy: "The which if your honourable Lordship shall accept," writes he of his *Apuleius*, "and take in good part, I shall not only thinke my small travell and labour well employed, but shall also receive a further comfort to attempt some more serious matter."

If the serious matter were ever attempted, its very gravity has sunk it out of knowledge: unless Adlington be the author of that very rare and exceeding obvious tract in verse, entitled, *A Speciall Remedie against the force of lawlesse Love.*† This was published

* The first edition was "imprinted at London in Fleet Streate at the Signe of the Oliphante by Henry Wykes, Anno 1566." Other editions appeared in 1571, 1582 (the rarest), 1596, 1600 and 1639.

† The full title runs thus: "A Speciall Remedie against the furious force of lawlesse Love. And also a true description of the same. With our delightfull devices of daintie delightes to

in 1579, and ascribed upon the title-page to W. A. As the agreement of name and date is perfect, so also the tone of the preface corresponds precisely with Adlington's admonition to the reader of *The Golden Asse.* When the friendly reader of the *Speciall Remedie* is warned "how like unto a beast love transformeth a man, during the which nothing can be exercised in minde, nothing by reason or study of minde can be done," you are forthwith reminded of Apuleius, and of Lucius changed to an ass. The verses are properly forgotten, but by his own confession we know him subject to an invincible morality which, ill according with his century, drove him perchance to undertake this enterprise, gloomy enough for oblivion. "Lector intende: laetaberis;" such is the bidding of Apuleius. And Adlington apologises that "although the matter seeme very light and merry, yet the effect thereof tendeth to a good and vertuous moral," just as the author of the *Speciall Remedie* remarks with Plinie, "there is no book so simple, but that therein is somewhat worthy the noating." As though the Milesian Tale were judged, not by its pleasantry and delight, but by the quality of its moral sustenance!

But Adlington was of those who would allegorise

passe away idle time, with pleasure and profit. Newly compiled in English verse by W. A. Imprinted by Richard Jhones, and are to be sold at his shop over against S. Sepulchres Church without Newgate, 1579." The tract, which is unique, was found in the Evidence Room in Northumberland House, and reprinted in 1844 by the Roxburghe Society.

both mythology and romance. The fall of Icarus is an example to proud and arrogant persons that "weeneth to climbe up to the heavens;" and further, he holds that "by Mydas is carped the foul sin of Avarice." And as if to excuse the translation of a "meere jeast and fable," he addresses to the reader the most solemn homily, setting forth the example of Nebuchadnezzar and upholding the efficacy of prayer. "Verily under the wrap of this transformation is taxed the life of mortall men," thus he writes in the proper spirit of the divine; "concluding that we can never bee restored to the right figure of ourselves, except we taste and eat the sweet Rose of reason and vertue, which the rather by mediation of praier we may assuredly attaine." Nor is this the mere perversion of ingenuity. His prudery is perfectly sincere. In many places he is inclined, by a modest suppression, to mitigate the gaiety of the Apuleian narrative. But only once he completely sacrifices his author's effect to his own scruples; and the restrained nobility of his prose more than atones for lack of scholarship and a prudish habit of mind. The lapse of three centuries has left his book as fresh and living as its original, and withal as brave a piece of narrative as the literature of his century has to show.

HERONDAS

HERONDAS

BOOKS, says Hazlitt, are not like women, the worse for being old. But the most of men, loving the crude better than the mellow, would cheerfully surrender the Classics, three-fifths of which America has condemned as "very filthy trash," for the last sensation of the circulating library. Perhaps it is the spirit of optimism which compels this eager interest in the newest literature. Upon so vast a rubbish-heap, whispers Hope, surely some pearls may lie concealed. And then how pleasant a satisfaction is it to forestall your neighbour, to discourse familiarly of a modern masterpiece, which has eluded a rival's vigilance! Reading is pursued less for its own sake than from the lust of discovery. Nowadays genius must e'en divide the honours with its Columbus, and not a few critics affect to believe that, if they did not actually create the works which they "first introduced to the public," at least they have the sole right to appraise them. What doth it profit us to read Shakespeare or Balzac? In their works there is no monopoly. He who knows them not must needs in very shame feign their acquaintance. So ancient volumes—in letters ten years are as a thousand—are imprisoned, like criminals or paupers, in the gloomy dungeon of a library, while the common novel enjoys the larger freedom of Mudie's and the bookstall. And shriller and shriller rises the voice of Boston, proclaiming that before it all was chaos.

The *Mimes* of Herondas, the treasure brought to light some years since in the British Museum, should gratify a double taste. Two thousand years old, they are as young as yesterday. Though they have survived the searching test of time, they have been unseen of mortal eyes for countless centuries. Pliny, with perhaps a suspicion of recklessness, praised their elegance and charm ("humanitas et venustas"), and yet if you buy Mr. Kenyon's transcription, with your own paper-knife you may separate their virgin pages. The few short dialogues, thus revealed to us, will keep the critics busy for years to come. The lexicon must extend shelter to their ἅπαξ εἰρημένα; their disorderly perfects will be placed upon trial before a jury of grammarians, while he whom no grammatical licence can terrify will see in the *Mimes* of Herondas the revelation of a lost *genre* as well as a vivid and familiar image of ancient life. Even in the golden age of Greek literature the mime was practised and esteemed. The works of Sophron, the master of the form, have followed Menander and Sappho into the night of forgetfulness. Yet it is their glory to have won the admiration of Plato, whose last hours they soothed, and who is said to have died with a copy beneath his pillow. A few poor fragments and half a dozen titles are all that remain, and of Sophron no more may be said than that he wrote a kind of rhythmic prose or Whitmanian verse, and that he pictured the characters of his contemporaries and the habit of their lives in dramatic dialogues.

But there is nothing new under the sun, and the recovery of Herondas proves beyond dispute that the long-lost mime is still handled with success, that it is indeed none other than that dialogue which to-day threatens the supremacy of the novel. The resemblance is more than superficial. In either case the medium is the same. The favourite theme of Herondas, as of his unconscious imitators, is the passion and frivolity of women, and he treats it with a verve and freedom after which the moderns limp in vain. So the suggestion that the *Mimes* were intended for dramatic representation appears ridiculous. Assertion must be backed by overwhelming evidence before so preposterous an opinion may be entertained. To bury these dainty pictures of life and character beneath the machinery of the stage were too shameless an outrage upon the proprieties, which the Greek temperament was wont to respect. Unless the Young Reciter were as deadly a blight upon the ancient as upon the modern world, the lines of Herondas can scarce have been spoken in public. Imagine *The Jealous Woman* performed with the pomp and circumstance of scenic display! The mere suggestion is blasphemy.

For the niceties of verse Herondas displays a perfect contempt. His metre—the choliambic—is more familiar than refined, and he has treated it with so licentious an asperity that it produces the effect of prose. It may be compared to the formless couplet wherein Reece and Blanchard were wont to enshrine their pearls of thought. The resemblance is merely external, as Herondas never stoops to the folly and dulness of those masters of burlesque. The diction is designedly undistinguished. In vain you look for coloured phrase or long-sought image. One expression —and one alone—lingers in the memory. In the sixth mime two ladies are discussing with infinite animation some mysterious implement, the handiwork of Cerdon, the leather-worker. "Its softness," says Coritto, in a moment of feminine enthusiasm, "is sleep itself" (ἡ μαλακότης ὕπνος). The phrase is elegant, and though it may have been borrowed from Theocritus, at any rate the application is original.

But if Herondas, in spite of Pliny's criticism, was not wont to polish and to refine his style, he had a marvellous talent for presentation. His characters breathe and live; his simple situations are sketched in a dozen strokes, but with so vivid a touch that they are perfectly realised. The material is drawn from the commonplace of life, but it is handled with so just a sense of reality that two thousand years have not availed to tarnish the truth of the picture. The book is as modern as though it had been written—not recovered—yesterday. The emotions which Herondas delineates are not Greek, but human, and no preliminary cramming in archæology is necessary for their appreciation. The student of Greek literature is so intimately accustomed to the austere pomp of tragedy, to the measured dignity of restrained prose, that he is apt to forget that those who spake the tongue which Sophocles wrote also lived an engrossing life of their own. You contemplate their masterpieces of art, and you dream that they paced through life apparelled ever in flowing robes, a finger upon their brow, as though they were still rapt in adoration of the ideal. And you open Herondas, and Gyllis apologises to Metriche for not having called before, but then they do live so far apart, and the roads are so muddy; or Metro and Coritto deplore the shortcomings of their servants, or a group of trippers gaze open-eyed at the glories of the temple of Asclepius. What can touch the sympathies more nearly than these sketches of life? Not even the most real of American realists could sniff therein the pitiful odour of romance or classicism. Their familiarity is, in a sense, more thrilling than the most exquisite verse. Here, indeed, is the Greek revealed in dressing-gown and slippers. The verisimilitude is heightened by the proverbs—or slang, if you will—wherewith the creations of Herondas enforce their meaning. "A ship," says Gyllis, pressing the temptation of Metriche, " is not safe on one cable;" while the same lady, in extolling the virtues of her champion, Gryllus, exclaims after Aristophanes: "he never moves a chip (οὐδὲ κάρφος κινέων); he never felt Cythera's dart." When the unhappy Battarus has received a thrashing at Thales' hands, he tells the jury he "suffered as much as a mouse in a pitch-pot." Thus spake the ancients, and thus might the men and women speak of to-day. As the world was never young, so it will never grow old. The archæologist devotes years of research to compiling a picture of Greek life, and the result is *Charicles*—a solid and unrelieved mass of "local colour." The life and exploits of a generation are ruthlessly ascribed to one poor youth, who must needs crowd every hour of his life, that no custom be left without its illustration. There is no proportion, no atmosphere, no background, so that all is false save the details, which merely overload the canvas. Herondas, on the other hand, presents not a picture, but an impression; and one mime reveals more of life as it was lived two thousand years ago than the complete works of Becker, Ebers, and the archæologists.

Metriche and Gyllis, who conduct the first dialogue, might have walked straight out of (or into) the ribald page of *la Vie Parisienne*. Theocritus has handled the same situation—a morning call—but then he was a poet, and carried the mime off with him to the skies. Metriche, the young wife of Mandris; Gyllis, an old lady; and Threissa, Metriche's maid, are the persons of the tiny drama, and thus it opens:

"*Metriche*. Threissa, there is a knock at the door; go and see if it is a visitor from the country.

"*Threissa*. Who's there?

"*Gyllis.* 'Tis I.

"*Threissa.* Who are you? Are you afraid to come any nearer?

"*Gyllis.* All right, you see, I am coming in.

"*Threissa.* What name shall I say?

"*Gyllis.* Gyllis, the mother of Philainium. Go indoors, and announce me to Metriche.

"*Threissa.* A caller, ma'am.

"*Metriche.* What, Gyllis, dear old Gyllis! Turn the chair round a little, girl. What fate induced you to come and see me, Gyllis? An angel's visit, indeed! Why, I believe it's five months since any one dreamt of your knocking at my door.

"*Gyllis.* I live far off, my dear, and the mud in the lane is up to your knees. I am no stronger than a fly, for old age is heavy upon me, and the shadow of death is at my side.

"*Metriche.* Cheer up! don't malign Father Time; you are strong enough yet to strangle others.

"*Gyllis.* Joke away; that's natural for girls like you, though joking won't stir your blood. But, my dear girl, what a long time you've been a widow. It's ten months since Mandris was despatched to Egypt, and he hasn't sent you a single line; doubtless he has forgotten you, and is drinking at a new spring. The house of the goddess is there. For in Egypt you may find all things that are or ever were—wealth, athletics, power, fine weather, glory, goddesses, philosophers, gold, handsome youths, the shrine of the god and goddess, the most excellent king, the finest museum in the world, wine, all the good things you can desire, and women, by Persephone, countless as the stars and beautiful as the goddesses that appealed to Paris."

So Gyllis, increasing her boldness, suggests that Mandris is dead, and reveals the purpose of her visit.

"Now listen to the news I have brought you after this long time. You know Gryllus, the son of Matachene, who was such a famous athlete at school, won a couple of prizes at Corinth when a youth, and remains to-day an eminent bruiser? Then he is very rich, and he leads the quietest life—a virgin seal, so help me Cytherea. Well, he saw you the other day in the procession of Misa, and was smitten to the heart. And, my dear girl, he never leaves my house day or night, but he bemoans his fate; he is positively dying of love. Now, my dear Metriche, for my sake do commit this one little sin. You will have a double joy. . . . Think it over, take my advice, he loves you."

Metriche is righteously indignant.

"By the fates, Gyllis, your white hairs blunt your reason. As I hope for the return of Mandris and the favour of our Lady Demeter, I shouldn't like to have heard this from another woman's lips. . . . And you, my dear, never come to my house with such proposals again. . . . For none may make mock of Mandris. But, if what the world says be true, I needn't speak to Gyllis like this. Threissa, let us have some refreshments; bring the decanter and some water, and give the lady something to drink. . . . Now, Gyllis, drink, and show that you aren't angry."

And so with a delightful interchange of civilities the quarrel is brought to an end. "The chatter of women," says the translator of Theocritus, "has changed no more in a thousand years than the song of birds."

The second mime is in a very different key. The scene is a law court, where Battarus, who pursues the pandar's ancient calling, brings an action against one Thales, a Phrygian plutocrat, a famous *rastaquoère*, for assault and battery. The plaintiff's speech is as admirable a specimen of Old Bailey tub-thumping as may be found outside the private orations of Demosthenes. "Deem not," exclaims the valiant Battarus, "that in protecting me you are guarding the interest of a poor pimp. No, the honour and independence of your city are at stake. I have been assaulted and robbed by one who is not a citizen, who is not even a man, but a Phrygian rascal—Artimmas was his name, though now he has the effrontery to call himself Thales. He thinks because he has a yacht and smart clothes that he is a gentleman with the privilege of assault. But your laws condemn him—your laws which protect even the slave from injury. Yet what should you, Thales, know of laws or cities—you who spend to-day at Bricindera, and are off towards Abdera to-morrow? I suffered as much as a mouse in the pitchpot. To cut a long story short, this Thales came to my house the other night, broke open my door, knocked me down, and carried off my Myrtale by force. Come here, Myrtale, show yourself to the court: don't be ashamed; imagine that the jury who face you are all brothers and fathers. See, gentlemen, how dishevelled she looks; that's all because this scoundrel dragged her off with intolerable violence. O, old age, had it not been for you, this ruffian should have spilt his blood! You laugh? I follow a disreputable trade —that I don't deny—and my name is Battarus, and my father Sisymbrus, and my grandfather Sisymbriscus (both inglorious names), were pandars before me, but Thales should treat me decently all the same. You, Thales, will object that you love Myrtale; well, I love porridge; give me the one and you shall have the other. Nay, if you wish it, Thales, I am ready to be put to the torture, but you must first deposit the penalty. When I ask you for a verdict, gentlemen, I am thinking not only of myself, but of all the strangers who take refuge in your city. You will show how great is Cos, how powerful Merops; you will declare the fame that belonged to Thessaly and to Hercules; you will relate how Asclepius came hither from Tricca, and how it was here that Phœbe gave birth to Leto. And it will do Thales good to be cast, for the more you beat a Phrygian the better he is, if the ancient proverb do not lie." And doubtless the jurymen of Cos found the flattery of Battarus, if not his eloquence, irresistible, and awarded a comfortable verdict. The speech, though it be not literature of the best kind, is an interesting document; and in the plaintiff's frank confession of his own iniquities, as in the exquisitely pompous peroration, there is even a touch of the sublime.

The scene shifts to the house of a schoolmaster, who is implored by an indignant mother to chastise her impudent good-for-nothing son. Flog him, she says, within an inch of his miserable life (ἄχρις ἡ ψυχὴ αὐτοῦ ἐπὶ χειλέων μοῦνον ἡ κακὴ λειφθῇ). The text is so corrupt that we can only form a vague opinion of the rascal's crimes. He has a taste for bad company and spends the livelong day in knuckle-bones, and when that seems too tame, he brings ruin on his mother's house with pitch-and-toss. Then "he positively refuses to work, and his wretched slate lies desolate in a corner, except when with a leer of destruction he rubs it all out. But his knuckle-bones are always polished and put away in their bag, brighter than the oil-jar, which we use for everything. And then he doesn't even know his alphabet unless one shouts it at him a dozen times. . . . Indeed I think I was a fool to teach him his letters, thinking he would be a prop for my old age, when he is only fit to feed donkeys. . . . And if we dare to scold, he won't cross the threshold for three days, and breaks his poor old mother's heart with anxiety, or he will sit astride the roof like a monkey and glare down at us. And that is not all. He breaks the tiles, so that when the winter comes, the neighbours have but one voice: 'Cottalus the son of Metrotime has been at his tricks again.' Stripe him black and blue, Lampriscus, as a Delian fisherman, who drags out his wretched life upon the sea." The schoolmaster is stern, as becomes his trade, and calls for his cow-hide. Poor Cottalus is unmercifully thrashed, and promises repentance between the blows, invoking the friendly Muses and his master's beard. But his mother is obdurate. "Take him away," says the schoolmaster to his slaves. "No, Lampriscus," shouts the mother, "don't leave off until the sun goes down." "He is far more mottled than a water-snake already," replies Lampriscus, and the boy is driven off to reflect in confinement upon his crimes and their punishment.

Far gayer in spirit is *The Visit to the Temple of Asclepius*. Here are two ladies laden with offerings who come to consult the god. The demands of piety once satisfied by a comprehensive prayer to Asclepius, and to all the gods and goddesses who cherish his hearth, they wander off to look at the statues which adorn the temple, and to express with confidence their innocent enthusiasm. They might be modern tourists at Westminister Abbey. "Dear, dear, friend Cynno," murmurs one, "do look at the beautiful statues. Whose work is that, and who set it up?" "The sons of Praxiteles were the sculptors," replies Cynno, "can't you see, it's written on the base? And Euthies, the son of Prexo, set it up. . . . But see the girl gazing at the apple. She will die on the spot if she doesn't get hold of it; and look at the boy strangling the goose! If it weren't made of stone you would say that he would speak in our very presence. Before very long, men will be able to put life into stones. Follow me, my dear, and I will show you such wonders as you have never seen in all your life." The art criticism, the same yesterday, to-day, and for ever, is interrupted by Cynno's altercation with her maid. "Go and fetch the verger!" screams the visitant. But the poor girl, overcome doubtless by the many splendours of the temple, merely stands gaping at her mistress. "She glares with an eye bigger than a crab's. Go and fetch the verger, I tell you!" Cynno's friend attempts to soothe the lady's frenzy. "She is a slave," she mutters, "and the ears of a slave are always slow." And even Cynno is pacified at last. "Stay," she cries, "the door is open and we can enter the chancel"; and again the ladies fall to art criticism. "You might think that Athene fashioned those beautiful works." "If I were to scratch this naked boy," replies the other, "don't you think I should leave a scar? And this cow, and the man leading it, and the woman who meets him, and that hook-nosed fellow, and the man with bristles on his forehead, aren't they lifelike?" "To be sure they are," says Cynno; "but then Apelles always is so realistic." These words are an echo of the country cousin at the Academy; but the verger approaches to declare that the ladies' sacrifice is acceptable and of a good portent, and to call down the blessing of the god upon them and their kin. Whereupon he is made happy by the drumstick—a cock was the offering; and it is only the payment in kind, which separates the drama from our own time.

But *The Jealous Woman* (ἡ ζηλότυπος) is Herondas' masterpiece. Its reality may only be matched in the most modern French literature.

There is a frank brutality in its subject which might have endeared it to M. de Maupassant, but so exquisitely is it handled, so justly is it proportioned, that its realism does not and cannot offend. Bitinna, an elderly lady, is madly jealous of Gastro, her favourite slave. She has caught him with Amphytaea, Meno's daughter, and the poor wretch sheepishly confesses that he "has seen" the girl his mistress mentions. Bitinna is furious, and Gastro replies with much dignity: "Bitinna, I am a slave; use me as you will, but do not suck my blood day and night"—a phrase which might have come from the very latest and most daring of French novels. However, Bitinna is not to be appeased. "It is I," says she, "who made you a man among men, and if I did wrong, you will not again find Bitinna the fool you think her." So in a frenzy she orders her favourite to be stripped and flogged—a thousand stripes on his back, a thousand on his belly, and bids her slaves drag him off to the punishment. "Bitinna," he pleads, "forgive me this once. I am but a man and I sinned. But if ever again you catch me doing what you do not wish, brand me." At length, after a torrent of altercation and abuse, she changes her mind and, resolving to brand him, bids Cosis to attend with his needles and his ink. Then Cydilla, a slave girl, intercedes for the miserable Gastro, and the hard heart of Bitinna is softened by the vapid argument that it is a Saint's day, and that the festival of the dead is approaching. "This time I will forgive you, but give your thanks to Cydilla here, whom I love as well as my own Batyllis, and whom I nursed with my own hands."

The *dénouement* is tame and trivial, and wholly unworthy of the spirited opening. But the fact that they do live happy ever after avails not to spoil a marvellously vivid and cruel picture of life. In Greek literature it is unsurpassed, and the world scarce realises yet how precious a treasure it has got in Herondas. There is not a single mime that has not a character and interest of its own. The others, difficult as they are, contain the most spirited passages. Coritto and Metro, for example, prattle with light-hearted vivacity of a disreputable object—*βαύβων* they call it—the work of an artist in leather, named Cerdo. Metro is burning to find the author of the masterpiece, and implores Coritto to tell her where he may be seen. At last Coritto is complaisant, and presently—in another mime—Metro pays the distinguished cobbler a visit. These three personages are realised with perfect conviction and more than a touch of malice. The corrupt Coritto, the eager, cunning Metro, the volubly insolent Cerdo will be familiar till the end of time. The fragments, moreover, are provoking in their incompleteness. There is enough left of *The Dream* to convince you that the farmer's indignant wife, who in a fury awakens her lazy slaves, bidding them drive the pig to pasture, would have been a portrait not unworthy its gallery. But, alas ! its conclusion is no better than a collection of inarticulate symbols.

Such, in brief outline, is the work of this long-forgotten poet. To have brought him once more to light is an achievement of which the British Museum may well be proud. The mimes are not statues of the fifth century, but rather exquisite terra-cottas, quaintly and daintily fashioned, such as prudery commonly withdraws from public exhibition, and softened by that touch of nature which makes fiction real, and renders the old new again. And it gives us good hope of the future. If Herondas be found, why not Sophron, or Menander, or the priceless Sappho herself? An unjust fate still hides the works of these artists from our gaze. But we have Herondas, and let us make the best of him. At any rate, he has proved that scholarship too may know the excitement of discovery.

EDGAR ALLAN POE

EDGAR ALLAN POE

IF Poe's life was a tangle of contradiction, his posthumous fame has been a very conflict of opposites. He has been elevated to heaven, he has been depressed to hell; he has been pictured angel and devil, drunkard and puritan. His poetry has seemed to this one the empty tinkling of a cymbal, to that the last expression of verbal beauty. But despite the warfare of opinions, he has been read and imitated throughout the world, and he is still, after half a century, the dominant influence of three literatures. An inventor in many fields, he deserves whatever homage may be paid him; and if his genius has been somewhat obscured by the monument, in ten volumes, which Chicago has erected to his honour, the zealot will discover many a block of pure marble, half hidden in the heap of shot rubble.

Poe in ten volumes! Did fortune ever play a more wayward trick upon a man? Poe in ten volumes—Poe, to whom a long poem was a flat contradiction! His editors omit nothing, who might have omitted so much. They spare you neither his casual reflections upon handwriting, nor his ephemeral portraits of America's forgotten *literati*. Did he, in the Forties, review such a piece of bookmaking as was not worth his momentary regard, it is at last set forth with the added dignity of enclosing covers. There is no doubt that he would have been shocked himself at this work of patient resurrection. Had he but lived to edit his own work, his fastidious care would assuredly have rejected the journalism and cut the final edition short by five volumes. Yet it were ungracious to reproach the piety of his editors. If you are indifferent to Poe's opinion of Christopher P. Cranch, you need not read it; and, having all, you are not harassed by the fear that you have been defrauded of a masterpiece.

No sooner was Poe dead than he became the immediate prey of the body-snatcher. The literary hyena fastened upon his corpse, and fattened hideously upon his desecrated blood. No poet, since Shelley, had given the ghoul so rich an opportunity. As the whole tragedy of Poe's life sprang from a hostile environment, so after his death the environing enemies leapt to their final act of resentment and revenge. He was a drunken monster, who had committed all the crimes invented in his gloomiest romances. *William Wilson* was a true page of autobiography; the brutalities of *The Black Cat* were among the slightest of his indiscretions; worse even, *teste* Gilfillan, he murdered his wife that he might find a suitable motive for *The Raven!* Now, if Gilfillan had read the works of his victim, he would have known that realism was loathsome to the temperament of Poe, who had no need to rehearse his effects. But when the slanderer is abroad, he cares not how flagrant are his calumnies, especially if he speak in the cause of morality. Stupidity's true mouthpiece, however, was one Rufus Griswold, who easily outgilfillaned the smug Gilfillan himself. This vessel of wrath had been the poet's friend, and (strange to tell) Poe, by appointing him his literary executor, was unconsciously guilty of posthumous suicide. Griswold was not one to lose an illegitimate occasion. Poe died on October 8, 1849. On October 9 Griswold's infamy was in type. Hate and malice scream in every line of this monumental hypocrisy. Here speaks, through the mouth of Griswold, the hungry middle-class, which hated poetry and loathed the solitary dignity of Poe. The poet's character, said this literary Pecksniff, was "shrewd and naturally unamiable." He recognised no "moral susceptibilities"; he knew "little or nothing of the true point of honour." His one desire was to "*succeed*—not shine, not serve—succeed, that he might have the right to despise a world which galled his self-conceit." And so magnificently did he "succeed," so vilely did he sacrifice his art to prosperity, that America, which kept Griswold in affluence, condemned the author of *William Wilson* to starvation and neglect!

But Griswold's purple patch must be given in its true colour. In these terms did our moralist describe the friend, laid but a few hours since in the grave: "Passions, in him, comprehended many of the worst emotions which militate against human happiness. You could not contradict him but you raised quick choler; you could not speak of wealth but his cheek paled with gnawing envy. The astonishing natural advantages of this poor boy—his beauty, his readiness, the daring spirit that breathed around him like a fiery atmosphere—had raised his constitutional self-confidence into an arrogance that turned his very claims to admiration into prejudices against him. Irascible, envious—bad enough, but not the worst, for these salient angles were all varnished over with a cold, repellent cynicism; his passions vented themselves in sneers." Those there are who assert that Griswold's outrage upon truth and taste was a revenge, deliberately taken upon Poe's hostile criticism. But there is no need to spy out a motive for so simple a crime. Griswold spoke not for himself, but for his world. Genius is repellent to those who know it not; gaiety is a crime in the eyes of unhappier men who fear not the disease. The envious morality of hypocrites, in whose veins vinegar flows for blood, rises superior to all the obligations of taste and friendship. No doubt the infamous Rufus laid down his pen that day with infinite content; no doubt he adjusted his spectacles over the *Tribune* next morning with a more than usual placidity. Thus he, who would not allow a poet the licence of displeasure, gives an easy rein to his own denunciation. Nor does the poor devil divine the incongruity. Poe's "harsh experience," he says in a tone of grievance, "had deprived him of all faith in man or woman." Of course it had: Poe had known Griswold.

But all the world was not as Griswold. Willis was quick to champion the dead man, and to declare that he had always been for him an exemplar of amiability. Indeed, there is a cloud of witnesses to prove not only the cowardice of Griswold, but his untruth. To Mrs. Osgood Poe was never "otherwise than gentle, generous, well-bred, and fastidiously refined." The intelligent few among his contemporaries understood him, at least by flashes, and did not apply to him the rigorous code of a magistrate trying a drunken navvy. To visit him at his house (you are told) was to be convinced of his refinement and simplicity. There was one friend who found this envious monster devoting himself to the care of birds and flowers. And, strangest irony of all, Mrs. Whitman, whom Poe's enemies assert to have endured the worst affront, proved the noblest and most eloquent of his champions. Had not the shriek of malice been raised so often, Poe's character might be left to defend itself. His works are ours; his opinions are familiar, if not accepted; the music of his verse still sings in our ear. But the dishonour done to his memory compels a defence, especially since the very simplicity of his character exposed him to affront. There should, then, be no uncertainty in a benign judgment. Some men, says Baudelaire, have *guignon* written upon their forehead, and Edgar Poe was of their number. He was born out of time, out of place. He was bidden to live in an alien and a hostile world, whence he recoiled in an impotent horror. A poet whose intelligence was solitary and aloof, he was driven into the battle-field, and it is not surprising that he suffered irremediable defeat at the hands of the Griswolds of his time. His life was always a dream, often a nightmare; and, since he lived shut up within himself, he knew not envy, but merely contempt. How should he be envious of the contemporaries whom he surpassed? Despite his melancholy, he enjoyed those periods of sanguine expectation which are proper to his temperament. For instance, he preserved a fervent faith in *The Stylus*, that imagined review which should reform American literature and fill his pocket. The exemplary burgess denounced him for a drunkard and a sloth, forgetting, in his hasty censure, that Poe was not only devoted to his family and friends, but that in sixteen years he produced a greater sum of admirable work than any octogenarian in America.

He was an idealist, caught up into a real world; he was a poet stifled in an atmosphere of commerce and morality; he was a Southerner in the midst of Abolitionists; he was a lofty aristocrat living in an unbridled democracy. His very beauty, the charm of his voice, the quiet distinction of his manner, his love of splendour, of noble houses, and Italian gardens—all these qualities aroused the suspicion of his contemporaries. His years of travel, his swiftly garnered experience had given him that air of a "gentleman" which is seldom beloved in a progressive state. Though it is ever hazardous to confuse a writer with his work, yet one may believe that in *The Domain of Arnheim* Ellison's ideals are Poe's own. Little enough have they to do with citizenship or a liberal franchise. Here they are—(1) free exercise in the open air; (2) the love of woman; (3) the contempt of ambition; (4) the conviction that attainable happiness is in proportion to its spirituality. Naturally Griswold found nothing in these aspirations save arrogance and contempt.

But Poe, in a letter to Lowell, has best described his own temperament. "I am excessively slothful and wonderfully industrious," he said, "by fits." He denies that he is ambitious, unless negatively. "I really perceive," goes on the passage of self-revelation, "that vanity about which most men merely prate—the vanity of the human or temporal life. I live continually in a reverie of the future. I have no faith in human perfectibility. I think that human exertion will have no appreciable effect upon humanity." How should a poet frank enough to formulate these truths, a poet whose life was "whim, impulse, passion, a longing for solitude, a scorn of all things present"—how should he appeal to the sympathy of his age or even to the bluff optimism of Mr. Lowell?

But the dullard's heaviest artillery has been marshalled against the crime of drunkenness. The poet's life is—in this aspect—a series of iterated and repelled charges. Yet the most that has been proved against Poe is that wine had an instant and perverse effect upon his brain. Let the dullard go home and thank God for that superior virtue which permits him to drink his muddy beer in peace; let him also reflect that no wine could purchase for him the dreams, the poems, the hopes which it purchased for Poe. That his death was tragic and premature is, alas! indisputable. And here, again, has been an occasion for much foolishness. He died, like Marlow and many another man of genius, in the street, unheeded, almost unrecognised. But he died at his own time, when his work was done, a victim to the stolid stupidity of circumstance. He was great, not on account of his frailty, which the foolish sometimes mistake for talent, but in his frailty's despite; and he yields not in good fortune to the mirror of respectability, whose sole congratulation is that his unremembered and useless life trickles out amiably in bed.

It is strangely ironical that though he would have chosen to live in the Kingdom of Fancy, he was driven at the outset to a picturesque activity. His descent was distinguished, yet he was little better than a foundling when he was adopted into the family of John Allan, who brought him up in gentle affluence. His education was varied and efficient. Two years spent at Stoke Newington, at the school of Dr. Bransby, gave him the local colour for *William Wilson*, and a hint for the description of that veritable "palace of enchantment," wherein his unhappy hero met his conscience. Thereafter he returned to America, spent a year without profit at the University of Virginia, and presently, following the example of his admired Coleridge, enlisted as a private soldier. Lowell relates, without a definite authority, that Poe had already set forth to fight at Byron's side for the independence of Greece, and that, having got into trouble at St. Petersburg, he was rescued by the American Consul. For the sake of romance you are willing to believe the legend, and you regret that fortune had not favoured the brave so far as to bring Poe into the presence of Byron. But at least it is true that Poe served three years in the United States Army, meanwhile, like Cumberbatch, cultivating the Muses. Then it was that Allan performed his last service. Having found a substitute, he entered him, though already disqualified by years, as a cadet at West Point. But West Point was as little to his mind as the barrack, and it was not long before a breach of discipline procured his dismissal. He published his poems by subscription among the cadets, and having no more to expect from his benefactor, he determined upon the profession of letters.

His first success was achieved (in 1833) with *The MS. found in a Bottle*, which won a prize offered by *The Saturday Visiter*. Henceforth, with varying fortune, he earned his living by his pen. He wrote stories, satires, poems ; his criticism became the terror of the incompetent ; and since his Southern descent, his genius, his reasonable contempt, rendered him unpopular in the North, he was, many years before his death, the best hated and most highly respected of his kind. The one constant ambition of his life

—to start a magazine of his own—was disappointed; but alone of his contemporaries he captured a reputation in Europe, and neither ill-health nor misfortune shook for an instant his legitimate confidence in himself, his determination to set in their place the pigmies who surrounded him. Meanwhile, his strange marriage with Virginia Clemm, who at the ceremony was not yet fourteen, and his unfailing devotion to his fragile wife and her mother, disproved the boorish cruelty wherewith he was so complacently charged. On the other hand, the affection, requited yet unsuccessful, which he cherished at the end for Mrs. Whitman, for "Annie," and for Mrs. Shelton, does not suggest the humour of one who had a strong, rational hold upon existence. But he lived his own life, as he died his own death, and it is for the Griswolds to hold their peace in the presence of genius.

At least his works remain to confute the blasphemer, and it is certain that no writer ever bequeathed so many examples to posterity. Although he went not beyond the tradition of his time, although he owed something to Maturin and Mrs. Radclyffe, something also, in decoration and decay, to the *romantiques* of 1830, he was essentially an inventor. He touched no kind of story without making it a type for all time. Even *The Narrative of Arthur Gordon Pym*, which you confess to be tiresome and elaborate, has been a stimulus to a whole generation of romance-mongers; and you feel, despite its faults, that it displays a greater verisimilitude, if not a greater knowledge, than the best of its successors. Before all things, Poe had the faculty of detaching himself from the present and of imagining unseen continents. With seamanship, science, erudition, mysticism, with all the branches of human knowledge he feigned an acquaintance. He tells you with pride that *The MS. Found in a Bottle* was written many years before he had seen the maps of Mercator; and you find yourself eagerly forgiving the amiable pedantry of his confession.

But it is in *The Tales of the Grotesque and Arabesque* that Poe first revealed his personal imagination—an imagination rather of tone than of incident. *The House of Usher*, *Ligeia*, and the rest surpass all other stories in economy of method and suggestion. Death, catalepsy, and the supernatural are the material of them all. They know neither time nor place; they are enwrapped in an atmosphere only substantial enough to enclose phantoms; ghostly castles frown upon sombre tarns, destined to engulph them; clouds, fantastically outlined, chase one another across a spectral sky; ancient families totter to their doom, overwhelmed in misery and disease; ruined halls are resplendent with red lanterns and perfumed with swinging censers; the heroine's hand is cold as marble, marble-cold also is her forehead, but she is learned in all the sciences, and the castle library contains the works of Cælius Secundus Curio and Tertullian. Everywhere there is a sombre splendour, a forbidding magnificence. No wonder that the dweller in an English abbey shudders at "the Bedlam patterns of the carpets of tufted gold." Naught save the names, which are of no country and of no age, heightens the colour of the monotone romance. Madeleine, Berenice, Ligeia, Morella, Eleonora—do they not echo the strangest harmonies, and by their beauty make more horrible the cold tragedy of their deaths? To analyse these fantasies closely is impossible; you must leave them to the low, dim-tinted atmosphere wherein Poe has enveloped them. They are vague, fleeting, mystical, perverse—a sensation of tapestry, whereon luminous figures wander hand in hand. Silence and horror are their cult, and there is not one of these ladies whose ever-approaching death would not be hastened by a breath of reality.

Ligeia dwells in "a dim and decaying city by the Rhine," but who would seek to discover her habitation? It were as infamous as to search beneath a tropical sun for "the Valley of the Many-coloured Grass," where pined the hapless Eleonora. The best of these fancies, in truth, are rather poetry than prose, and it was in their prose that Poe perfected his artifice of refrain. A sonorous passage in *Eleonora* is repeated with the stateliest effect, and the horror of *Silence* is increased tenfold by the oft-recurring phrase: "And the man trembled in the solitude, but the night waned, and he sat upon the rock." In these grotesque imaginings even laughter becomes a terror. At Sparta, says the monster of *The Assignation*, "the altar of Laughter survived all the others," and he chuckles at the very point of death. When, in *The Cask of Amontillado*, the last stone is fitted to Fortunato's living tomb, "there came from out the niche a low laugh," which might well have sent Montresor's hair on end. Not even did Morella's lover meet his doom with tears. "I laughed with a long and bitter laugh," he says, "as I found no trace of the first in the charnel where I laid the second—Morella." But, worst of all, the demon laughs when the whole world is cursed to silence: wherefrom you may deduce as sinister a theory of the ludicrous as you please.

And then he turned to another kind, and created at a breath M. Dupin, that master of insight, who proved that the complex was seldom profound, and who discovered by the natural transition from a colliding fruiterer, through street stones, stereotomy, Epicurus, and Dr. Nicholls, to Orion, that Chantilly was a very little fellow, and would do better for the Théâtre des Variétés. Now, Monsieur Charles A. Dupin is of good family—so much you are ready to believe; he is also young—a statement you decline to accept on the word of a creator, unless, indeed, he be the Wandering Jew. But whatever his age and breeding, he is a master of analysis, and plays at ratiocination as a boy plays with a peg-top. He knows by long experience that in pitting your intelligence against another's you are sure to win if you identify yourself with your adversary. And when once this principle is understood, it is as easy as a game of marbles, and more profitable. M. Dupin loves darkness better than light, not because his deeds are evil, but because, being a poet and a mathematician, he works better by lamp-light. Hence it is his practice to live through the day by the glimmer of two flickering candles, and to walk abroad at night under the spell of the gas-lamps. But if his work be serious, or if he be forced to interview the doltish Prefect of Police, then he sits in the dark, and silently puffs his meerschaum.

The smallest indication was sufficient for him, and while the police fumbled over the murders in the Rue Morgue, arresting a harmless bank-clerk, he not only discovered the true culprit, but was convinced that the culprit's master was a sailor, belonging to a Maltese vessel. "How was it possible?" asked his incredulous accomplice, "that you should know the man to be a sailor, and belonging to a Maltese vessel?" "I do not *know* it," said Dupin. "I am not *sure* of it! Here, however, is a small piece of ribbon, which from its form, and from its greasy appearance, has evidently been used in tying the hair in one of those long *queues* of which sailors are so fond. Moreover, this knot is one which few besides sailors can tie, and is peculiar to the Maltese." Imagine the joy of happening upon this masterpiece of combined observation and analysis, in the days before the trick had not been vulgarised beyond recognition! And yet, despite this flash of genius, M. Dupin affected to despise ingenuity, which he regarded as the cheapest of human qualities; and he would persuade you that all his finest effects were produced by pure reason! His most daring deed was done in the Rue Morgue: the instant discovery of the inhuman murderer was adroitness itself; and the advertisement of the recovered Ourang-Outang was even more brilliant. Unhappily there is a touch of melodrama in the locked door, the pistol upon the table, and the extorted confession. But M. Dupin is seldom guilty of such an indiscretion, and you readily forgive him. A more subtle achievement was the recovery of the purloined letter, for in this exploit he opposed the great Minister D——, and proved the superior at all points. In brief, his shining qualities are as stars in the night, nor have they been dimmed by the flickering rushlights of the unnumbered imitators, who mimic the tone of the inimitable Dupin.

Though *The Gold Bug* is a masterpiece of another sort, it is nearly related to *The Purloined Letter*. It displays the perfect logic, the complete lucidity, the mastery of analysis, which make M. Dupin immortal. No step in the adventure but is foreseen and inevitable. Never before nor since has use so admirable been made of ciphers and buried treasure. The material, maybe, was not new, but the treatment, as of a glorified problem in mathematics, was Poe's own invention. In his hands the slightest incident ceased to be curious, and became (so to say) a link in the chain of fate. Not only was he unrivalled in the art of construction, but he touched the simplest theme with a clairvoyant intelligence, which seemed at the same moment to combine and analyse the materials of his story. Thus, also, the best of his scientific parables convince the imagination, even if they leave the reason refractory.

But the purpose of these is too obvious, their central truths are too heavily weighted with pretended documents, for immortality. It is upon the grotesque, the horrible, and the ingenious that Poe has established his reputation. And surely the author of *Ligeia*, of *Silence*, of *William Wilson*, of the Dupin Cycle, of *The Gold Bug*, and of *The Mask of the Red Death* need not defend his title to undying fame.

Though Poe was a maker of great stories, he was not a great writer. That he might have been is possible, for none ever showed in fragments a finer sense of words; that he was not is certain. An American critic would excuse him upon the ground that he lived before Pater, Flaubert, and Arnold. Never was a more preposterous theory formulated. As though the art of prose were newly invented! The English tongue, accurate, noble, coloured, is centuries older than Pater; and even in Poe's own time there were models worth the following. He knew Coleridge from end to end, and did not profit by his example. So conscious is he of style in others, that he condemns the Latinity of Lamb, but he rarely knits his own sentences to perfection. The best he wraps round with coils of useless string, and he is not incapable of striking false notes upon the Early-Victorian drum. He shocks you, for instance, by telling you that William Wilson at Oxford "vied in profuseness of expenditure with the haughtiest heirs of the wealthiest earldoms in Great Britain"—a sentence equally infamous whether it appeal to the ear or to the brain. Egeaus, again, the ghoulish lover of Berenice, boasts, with a pride which Mrs. Radclyffe might envy, that "there are no towers in the land more time-honoured than my gloomy, grey, hereditary halls." This is fustian, and you regret it the more because in construction, in idea, Poe was seldom at fault. The opening of his stories is commonly perfect. How could you better the first page of *The House of Usher*, whose weird effect is attained throughout by the simplest means? Another writer would take five pages to explain what Poe has suggested in the first five lines of *The Oval Portrait*; and to how many has this rejection of all save the essential been a noble example? But Poe, writing on the impulse of a whim, let the style which he knew elude his grasp, and if his carelessness cast a shadow upon his true masterpieces, it reduces the several volumes of properly forgotten fantasies to the level of journalism.

The criticism of Poe inaugurated a new era, a new cult of taste and beauty. Whether in theory or in practice he was ahead not only of his time, but of all time. That same keen intelligence which created M. Dupin, tore to pieces the prevailing superstitions and disclosed in a few pages the true qualities of literature. Beauty is his cult; poetry for him is "the rhythmical creation of beauty." He is neither preacher nor historian. Being an artist, he esteems facts as lightly as morals. Art, he says, has "no concern whatever either with Duty or with Truth." A poem is written solely for the poem's sake. "Perseverance," again, "is one thing, genius quite another;" and the public has as little to do with the industry as with the inspiration of the artist. To us who have lived through the dark age of naturalism his passage upon Truth rings like a prophecy: "The demands of Truth," he writes in *The Poetic Principle*, "are severe; she has no sympathy with the myrtles. All *that* which is so indispensable in Song, is precisely all *that* with which *she* has nothing whatever to do. It is but making her a flaunting paradox to wreath her in gems and flowers." Even more precise and bitter is his epigrammatic indictment of Realism. "The defenders of this pitiable stuff"—you will find the lines in *Marginalia*—"uphold it on the ground of its truthfulness. Taking the thesis into question, the truthfulness is the one overwhelming defect. An original idea that—to laud the accuracy with which the stone is hurled that knocks us in the head. A little less accuracy might have left us more brains. And here are critics absolutely commending the truthfulness with which only the disagreeable is conveyed! In my view, if an artist must paint decayed cheeses, his merit will lie in their looking as little like decayed cheeses as possible." And that was written twenty years before the advent of Zola!

In *The Philosophy of Composition*, moreover, he explains, what should never have needed explanation, that a work of art is the result not of accident but of a reasoned artifice; and he illustrates his thesis by a whimsical, far-fetched analysis of his own *Raven*. He treats the poem with the same impartial intelligence which M. Dupin would have brought to the detection of a murderer or the discovery of a missing trinket. He was, in truth, the Dupin of Criticism. For he looked, with his keen eye and rapid brain, through the innumerable follies wherewith literature was obscured, and he rejected the false hypotheses as scornfully as M. Dupin set aside the imbecilities of the Prefect. As a censor of his contemporaries, he dipped his pen in gall. His sense of honour knew neither civility nor favouritism. Alone among critics he has come forth with a chivalrous defence of that craft, in which he took a fierce and lawful pride. He was no adulator ready-made to serve a Society of Authors: he was a judge, condemning the guilty with an honourable severity. "When we attend less to authority," he wrote, "and more to principles, when we look *less* at merit and *more* at demerit, we shall be better critics than we are." Is that not enough to make the Popular Novelist turn green with fury, especially since it is the deliberate utterance of a man whose example has furnished forth a whole library of popular novels? Twice he quotes the parable of the critic who "presented to Apollo a severe censure upon an excellent poem. The god asked him for the beauties of the work. He replied that he only troubled himself about the errors. Apollo presented him with a sack of unwinnowed wheat, and bade him pick out the chaff for his pains." Now, this is the critic's severest condemnation, and yet Poe defends his trade with an honourable loyalty: he is not sure, says he, that the god was in the right.

Being a severe judge, he was generously misunderstood. Longfellow was magnanimous enough to attribute "the harshness of his criticism to the irritation of a sensitive nature, chafed by some indefinite sense of wrong." Thus the illiterate are wont to ascribe the lightest censure to a critic's envy. And they do not see, neither Longfellow nor the illiterate, that they are bringing superfluous charges of bad faith. Is it possible that Longfellow could not imagine the necessity of censure? Is it possible that he, like the bleating lambs of fiction, believed that criticism is written, not for its own sake, but for the voidance of gall? If such were his creed, if he, being a critic, would never have written a line unblotted by hatred or irritation, it is fortunate that he did not lapse from his devotion to poetry. But Poe was not always harsh, and when he used the scourge, he used it in defence of his craft. It was his misfortune to review his contemporaries; and they, though they resented his reproach, have already justified his severity by crawling, one and all, into oblivion. A bold judgment, indeed, would suppress these innumerable pages of books reviewed—pages which served their turn at the moment, and which dimly reflect the brilliant insight of *Marginalia*. But when Poe encountered a master, he was eager in appreciation. His praise of Alfred Tennyson was as generous as it was wise. "In perfect sincerity," he wrote, "I regard him as the noblest poet that ever lived." And, again, remembering that this was written in 1843, you recognise in Poe the gift of prophecy.

But to complete the cycle of his accomplishments he was also a poet, and it is as a poet that he wears the greenest bays. Here his practice coincided accurately with his theory. He believed that a long poem was a contradiction in terms, and he only erred once against the light when he called *Eureka*, a tedious treatise upon all things and nothing, "a prose poem." In his eyes the sole aim of poetry was beauty, and such beauty as should touch the ear rather than the brain. His musical art eludes analysis, and he esteemed it great in proportion as it receded from the hard shapes and harder truths of life. Of him it might be said truly that "he seemed to see with his ear." You do not question *Annabel Lee* and *Ulalume*. You do not attempt to drag a common meaning from their gossamer loveliness. You listen to their refrains and repeated cadences; you delight in their rippling sound and subtle variations; and you are content to find yourself in the presence of an art which, like music, does not represent, but merely presents, an emotion. And because Poe acknowledged the artifice of his poetry, some have denied him imagination. But imagination most clearly manifests herself in artistic expression; and has naught in common with the rhymester's rolling eye and untutored fancy.

It is not surprising that Poe's multiform genius should have proved a dominant influence upon

European literature. Not only was he a sombre light to the decadence; not only was he a guiding flame in the pathway of the mystics; he also revived the novel of adventure and lost treasure, of the South Seas and of Captain Kidd. The atrocities which have been committed in the name of his Dupin are like the sands for number; and the detective of fact, as of romance, has attempted to model himself upon this miracle of intelligence. Thus he has been an example to both houses—to M. Huysmans, who has emulated his erudition, and to Gaboriau, who has cheapened his mystery. It is his unique distinction to have anticipated even the trivialities of life. His title, *The Man that Was Used up*, has let in upon us the legion of imbeciles who did or didn't, who would or wouldn't. He it was, too, that imagined the philosopher who, in the vanity of his heart, should spell his god with a little g! By a strange accident his influence came to us, not from America but from France. No sooner was *The Murders in the Rue Morgue* published in America, than it appeared as a *feuilleton* in *le Commerce*, and in 1846 was printed a volume of *Contes*, translated by Isabelle Meunier. Ten years later Baudelaire began the brilliant series of translations, which added the glory of Poe to French literature. That Poe gained in the transference there is no doubt: the looseness of his style was tightened in the distinguished prose of Baudelaire; and henceforth Poe was free to shape the literary future of France. So it was his example that moulded the *conte* to its ultimate completion. His talents of compression and facile exposition, his gift of building up a situation in a hundred words, were imitated by the army of writers who first perfected the short story, and then sent it across the Channel. Nor is Baudelaire the only poet who has turned Poe into French. M. Stéphane Mallarmé, also, has proved his sympathy with the author of *The Raven* in a set of matchless translations. He has changed the verse of Poe into a rhythmical prose, and withal he has kept so close to the original that the prose echoes not only the phrase but the cadence of the verse. And from France Poe penetrated every country in Europe. He is known and read in those remote corners which he described, yet never saw. He is as familiar in Spain as in Scandinavia, and *The Raven* has been translated "direct from English" in far-off Valparaiso.

And here is the final contrast of his life. The prophet of silence and seclusion is blown to the four winds of heaven. But he has conquered glory without stooping one inch from his proper attitude of aristocracy. He is still as exclusive and morose as his stories. Between him and his fantasies there is no discord. You imagine him always stern-faced and habited in black, with Virginia Clemm at his side, Virginia shadowy as Ligeia, amiable as the mild Eleonora in the Valley of the Many-coloured Grass. He dwelt in mid-America, and he was yet in fairyland. Though the squalor of penury and the magazines gave him neither "ancestral hall" nor "moss-grown abbey," he lived and died enclosed within the impregnable castle of his mind.

LUCIAN

I

LUCIAN*

I

IT is a commonplace of criticism that Lucian was the first of the moderns, but in truth he is near to our time, because of all the ancients he is nearest to his own. He was of those who made the discovery that there is material for literature in the debased and various life of every day—that to the seeing eye the individual is more wonderful in colour and complexity than the severely simple abstraction of the poets. He replaced the tradition, respected of his fathers, by an observation more vivid and less pedantic than the note-book of the naturalist. He set the world in the dry light of truth, and since the vanity of mankind is a constant factor throughout the ages, there is scarce a page of Lucian's writing that wears the faded air of antiquity. His personages are as familiar to-day as they were in the second century, because, with his pitiless determination to unravel the tangled skein of human folly, he never blinded his vision to their true

* Certaine Select Dialogues of Lucian together with his true Historie, translated from the Greeke into English by Mr. Francis Hickes. Printed by William Turner. 1634.

qualities. And the multiplicity of his interest is as fresh as his penetration. Nothing came amiss to his eager curiosity. For the first time in the history of literature (with the doubtful exception of Cicero) we encounter a writer whose ceaseless activity includes the world. While others had declared themselves poets, historians, philosophers, Lucian comes forth as a man of letters. Had he lived to-day, he would have edited a newspaper, written leading articles, and kept his name ever before the public in the magazines. For he possessed the qualities, if he avoided the defects, of the journalist. His phrase had not been worn by constant use to imbecility; his sentences were not marred by the association of commonness; his style was still his own and fit for the expression of a personal view. But he noted such types and incidents as make an immediate, if perennial, appeal, and to study him is to be convinced that literature and journalism are not necessarily divorced.

The profession was new, and with the joy of the innovator Lucian was never tired of inventing new genres. Romance, criticism, satire—he mastered them all. In *Toxaris* and *The Ass*, if indeed that work may be attributed to him, he proved with what delicacy and restraint he could handle the story. His hapless apprenticeship to a sculptor gave him the taste and feeling for art which he turned to so admirable an account. He was, in fact, the first of the art critics, and he pursued the craft with an easy unconsciousness of the heritage he bequeathed to the world.

Though he is silent concerning the technical practice of the Greeks; though he leaves us in profound ignorance of the art of Zeuxis, whose secrets he might have revealed had he been less a man of letters, he found in painting and sculpture an opportunity for elegance of phrase, and we would forgive a thousand shortcomings for such inspirations of beauty as the smile of Sosandra: τὸ μειδίαμα σεμνὸν καὶ λεληθὸς. In literary criticism he was on more familiar ground, yet here also he leaves the past behind. His knowledge of Greek poetry was profound; Homer he had by heart; and on every page he proves his sympathies by covert allusion or precise quotation. His treatise concerning the writing of history (Πῶς δεῖ ἱστορίαν συγγράφειν) preserves its force irresistible after seventeen centuries, nor has the wisdom of the ages impeached or modified this lucid argument. With a modest wit he compares himself to Diogenes, who, when he saw his fellow citizens busied with the preparations of war, gathered his skirts about him and fell to rolling his tub up and down. So Lucian, unambitious of writing history, sheltered himself from "the waves and the smoke," and was content to provide others with the best of good counsel. Yet such is the irony of accident that, as Lucian's criticism has outlived the masterpieces of Zeuxis, so the historians have snatched an immortality from his censure; and let it be remembered for his glory that he used Thucydides as a whip wherewith to beat impostors.

But matters of so high import did not always engross his humour, and in *The Illiterate Book-buyer* (Πρὸς τὸν ἀπαιδευτὸν καὶ πολλὰ βιβλία ὠνούμενον) he satirises a fashion of the hours and of all time with a courage and brutality which tear the heart out of truth. How intimately does he realise his victim! And how familiar is this same victim in his modern shape! You know the very streets he haunts; you know the very shops wherein he is wont to acquire his foolish treasures; you recognise that not by a single trait has Lucian dishonoured his model. In yet another strange instance Lucian anticipated the journalist of to-day. Though his disciples know it not, he invented the interview. In that famous visit to the Elysian Fields, which is a purple patch upon his masterpiece, *The True History*, he "went to talk with Homer the poet, our leisure serving us both well," and he put precisely those questions which the modern hack, note-book in hand, would seek to resolve. First, remembering the seven cities, he would know of Homer what fatherland claimed him, and when the poet "said indeed he was a Babylonian, and among his own countrymen not called Homer but Tigranes," Lucian straightly "questioned him about those verses in his books that are disallowed as not of his making;" whereto Homer replied with a proper condemnation of Zenodotus and Aristarchus. And you wonder whether Lucian is chastising his contemporaries or looking with the eye of a prophet into the future.

But even more remarkable than his many-coloured interest is Lucian's understanding. He was, so to say, a perfect intelligence thrown by accident into an age of superstition and credulity. It is not only that he knew all things: he saw all things in their right shape. If the Pagan world had never before been conscious of itself, it had no excuse to harbour illusions after his coming. Mr. Pater speaks of the intellectual light he turned upon dim places, and truly no corner of life escaped the gleam of his lantern. Gods, philosophers, necromancers yielded up their secrets to his inquiry. With pitiless logic he criticised their extravagance and pretension; and, actively anticipating the spirit of modern science, he accepted no fact, he subscribed to no theory, which he had not examined with a cold impartiality. Indeed, he was scepticism in human shape, but as the weapon of his destruction is always raillery, as he never takes either himself or his victims with exaggerated seriousness, you may delight in his attack, even though you care not which side wins the battle. His wit was as mordant as Heine's own—is it fantastical to suggest that Lucian too carried Hebrew blood in his veins?—yet when the onslaught is most unsparing he is still joyous. For a gay contempt, not a bitter hatred, is the note of his satire. And for the very reason that his scepticism was felt, that it sprang from a close intimacy with the follies of his own time, so it is fresh and familiar to an age that knows not Zeus. Not even the Dialogues of the Gods are out of date, for if we no longer reverence Olympus we still blink our eyes at the flash of ridicule. And might not the *Philopseudes*, that masterly analysis of ghostly terrors, have been written yesterday?

And thus we arrive at Lucian's weakness. In spite of its brilliance and flippancy, his scepticism is at times over-intelligent. So easy is it to extract sport from popular theology, that his ridicule of the Gods, exquisitely as it is expressed, sometimes suggests the odious pleasantry of the modern freethinker. His good sense baffles you by its infallibility; his sanity is so magnificently beyond question, that you pray for an interlude of unreason. The sprightliness of his wit, the alertness of his fancy, mitigate the perpetual rightness of his judgment. But it must be confessed that for all his delicate sense of ridicule he cherished a misguided admiration of the truth. If only he had understood the joy of self-deception, if only he had realised more often (as he realised in his stories) the delight of throwing probability to the winds, we had regarded him with a more constant affection. His capital defect sprang from a lack of the full-blooded humour which should at times have led him into error. And yet by an irony it was this very love of truth which suggested *The True History*, that enduring masterpiece of phantasy. Setting out to prove his hatred of other men's lies, he shows himself on the road the greatest liar of them all. "The father and founder of all this foolery was Homer's *Ulysses*:" thus he writes in his preface, confessing that in a spirit of emulation he "turned his style to publish untruths," but with an honester mind, "for this one thing I confidently pronounce for a truth, that I lie."

Such is the spirit of the work, nor is there the smallest doubt that Lucian, once embarked upon his voyage, slipped from his ideal, to enjoy the lying for its own sake. If *The True History* fails as a parody, that is because we care not a jot for Ctesias, Iambulus and the rest, at whom the satire is levelled. Its fascination, in fact, is due to those same qualities which, in others, its author affected to despise. The facile variety of its invention can scarce be matched in literature, and the lies are told with so delightful an unconcern, that belief is never difficult. Nor does the narrative ever flag. It ends at the same high level of falsehood in which it has its beginning. And the credibility is increased by the harmonious consistency of each separate lie. At the outset the traveller discovers a river of wine, and forthwith travels up stream to find the source, and "when we were come to the head" (to quote Hickes' translation), "no spring at all appeared, but mighty vine-trees of infinite number, which from their roots distilled pure wine, which made the river run so abundantly." So conclusive is the explanation, that you only would have wondered had the stream been of water. And how admirable is the added touch that he who ate fish from the river was made drunk! Then by a pleasant gradation you are carried on from the Hippogypians, or the Riders of

Vultures, every feather in whose wing is bigger and longer than the mast of a tall ship, from the fleas as large as twelve elephants, to those spiders of mighty bigness, every one of which exceeded in size an isle of the Cyclades. "These were appointed to spin a web in the air between the Moon and the Morning Star, which was done in an instant, and made a plain champaign, upon which the foot forces were planted."

Truly a very Colossus of falsehood, but Lucian's ingenuity is inexhausted and inexhaustible, and the mighty whale is his masterpiece of impudence. For he "contained in greatness fifteen hundred furlongs"; his teeth were taller than beech-trees, and when he swallowed the travellers, he showed himself so far superior to Jonah's fish, that ship and all sailed down his throat, and happily he caught not the pigmy shallop between his chops. And the geographical divisions of the whale's belly, and Lucian's adventures therein, are they not set down with circumstantial verity? Then there is the episode of the frozen ship, and the sea of milk, with its well-pressed cheese for an island, which reminds one of the Elizabethan madrigal: "If there were O an Hellespont of Cream." Moreover, the verisimilitude is enhanced by a scrupulously simple style. No sooner is the preface concerning lying at an end than Lucian lapses into pure narrative. A wealth of minutely considered detail gives an air of reality to the most monstrous impossibility; the smallest facts are explicitly divulged; the remote accessories described with order and impressiveness; so that the wildest invention appears plausible, even inevitable, and you know that you are in company with the very genius of falsehood. Nor does this wild diversity of invention suggest romance. It is still classic in style and form; not a phrase nor a word is lost, and expression, as always in the Classics, is reduced to its lowest terms.

But when the travellers reach the Islands of the Blessed, the style takes on a colour and a beauty which it knew not before. A fragrant air breathed upon them, as of "roses, daffodils, gillyflowers, lilies, violets, myrtles, bays, and blossoms of vines." Happy also was the Isle to look upon, *ἔνθα δή καὶ καθεωρῶμεν λιμένας τε πολλοὺς περὶ πᾶσαν ἀκλύστους καὶ μεγάλους, ποταμούς τε διαυγεῖς ἐξίοντας ἠρέμα ἐς τὴν θάλατταν· ἔτι δὲ λειμῶνας καὶ ὕλας καὶ ὄρνεα μουσικὰ, τὰ μὲν ἐπὶ τῶν ἠϊόνων ᾄδοντα, πολλὰ δε καὶ ἐπὶ τῶν κλάδων· ἀήρ τε κοῦφος καὶ εὔπνους περιεκέχυτο τὴν χώραν*: "a still and gentle air compassing the whole country." Where will you find a more vivid expression of serenity and delight? or where match "the melody of the branches, like the sound of wind instruments in a solitary place" (*ἀπὸ τῶν κλάδων κινουμένων τερπνά καὶ συνεχῆ μέλη ἀπεσυρίζετο ἐοικότα τοῖς ἐπ' ἐρημίας αὐλήμασι τῶν πλαγίων αὐλῶν*)? And when the splendour of the city breaks upon you, with its smaragdus, its cinnamon-tree, its amethyst, ivory and beryl, the rich babarity suggests Solomon's Temple, or the City of the Revelation. Its inhabitants are the occasion of infinite jesting, and again and again does Lucian satirise the philosophers, his dearest foes. Socrates was in danger of being thrust forth by Rhadamanthus, *ἤν φλυαρῆ καὶ μὴ εθέλῃ ἀφεὶς τὴν εἰρωνείαν εὐωχεῖσθαι*, while as for Diogenes the Sinopean, so profoundly was he changed from his old estate, that he had married Lais the Harlot.

The journey to Hell is another excuse to gird at the historians. The severest torments were inflicted, says Lucian, upon Ctesias the Cnidian, Herodotus and many others, which the writer beholding "was put in great hopes that I should never have anything to do there, for I do not know that ever I spake any untruth in my life." And yet with all his irony, all his scorn, Lucian has ever a side-glance at literature. The verse of Homer is constantly upon his lips, and it is from Homer that the gods take their ditties in the Elysian fields. Again, when the traveller visits the city of Nephelococcygia, it is but to think upon the poet Aristophanes, "how wise a man he was, and how true a reporter, and how little cause there is to question his fidelity for what he hath written."

Such is the work which, itself a masterpiece, has been a pattern and an exemplar unto others. If Utopia and its unnumbered rivals derive from Plato, there is not a single Imaginary Traveller that is not modelled upon Lucian. *The True History* was, in effect, the ancestor of a very full literature. Not only was its framework borrowed, not only was its habit of fantastic names piously imitated, but the disciples, like the master, turned their voyages to the purpose of satire. It was Rabelais, his speech emboldened by the frankness of his master, who made the first adaptation, for, while Epistemon's descent into Hell was certainly suggested by Lucian, Pantagruel's voyage is an ample travesty of *The True History*; and Lanterland, the home of the Lychnobii, is but Lychnopolis, Lucian's own City of Lights. The seventeenth century discovered another imitator in Cyrano de Bergerac, whose tepid *Voyage dans la Lune* is interesting merely because it is a link in the chain that unites Lucian with Swift. Yet the book had an immense popularity, and Cyrano's biographer has naught to say of the original traveller, save that he told his story "avec beaucoup moins de vraisemblance et de gentillesse d'imagination que M. de Bergerac." An astounding judgment surely, which time has already reversed. And then came *Gulliver's Travels*, incomparably the greatest descendant of *The True History*. To what excellent purpose Swift followed the lead of Lucian is proved alike by the amazing probability of his narrative and the cruelty of his satire. Like Lucian, he professed an unveiled contempt for philosophers and mathematicians; unlike Lucian, he made his imaginary journey the occasion for a fierce satire upon kings and politicians. But so masterly is the narrative, so convincing the reality of Lilliput and Brobdingnag, that Gulliver retains its hold upon our imagination, though the meaning of its satire is long since blunted. Swift's work came to astonish the world in 1727, and some fourteen years later in the century Holberg amazed the wits of Denmark with a satire cast in Lucian's mould. *Nicolai Klimii Iter Subterraneum*—thus ran the title; and from Latin the book was translated into every known tongue. The city of walking trees, the home of the Potuans, and many another invention, prove Holberg's debt to the author of *The True History*. Hereafter unnumbered Spaniards followed in the beaten track, while, though Fielding's *Journey to the Next World* is eclipsed by his novels, it still shows him a faithful imitator. And if the form is dead to-day, it is dead because the most intrepid humourist would hesitate to walk in the footsteps of Lemuel Gulliver.

Fortunate in his imitators, Lucian has been not wholly unfortunate in his translators. Not even envy could pick a quarrel with Francis Hickes, who first Englished *The True History*. The book appeared under the auspices of Hickes' son in 1634, four years after the translator's death. Thus it is described on the title-page: "Certaine Select Dialogues of Lucian together with his true Historie, translated from the Greeke into English by Mr. Francis Hickes. Whereunto is added the life of Lucian gathered out of his own Writings with briefe Notes and Illustrations upon each Dialogue and Booke, by T. H., Master of Arts, of Christ Church in Oxford. Printed by William Turner, 1634." Composed with a certain dignity, it is dedicated "to the Right Worshipful Dr. Duppa, Deane of Christ Church, and Vice-Chancellor of the famous Universitie in Oxford." And the work reflects a wholesome glory upon the famous University. For it is the work of a scholar, who knew both the languages. Though his diction lacked the spirit and colour which distinguish the more splendid versions of the Tudor age, he was far more keenly conscious of his original than his predecessors. Not only did he translate directly from the Greek, but he followed his original with loyalty and patience. In brief, his *Lucian* is a miracle of suitability. The close simplicity of Hickes fits the classical restraint of *The True History* to admiration. As the Greek is a model of narrative, so you cannot read the English version without thinking of the incomparable Hakluyt. Thirty years after the first printing of the translation, Jasper Mayne published his *Part of Lucian made English*, wherein he added sundry versions of his own to the work already accomplished by Francis Hickes. And in his *Epistle Dedicatory* he discusses the art of translation with an intelligence which proves how intimately he realised the excellent quality of Hickes' version. "For as the painter"—thus Jasper Mayne—"who would draw a man of a bald head, rumpled forehead, copper nose, pigge eyes, and ugly face, draws him not to life, nor doth the business of his art, if he draw him less deformed or ugly than he is; or as he who would draw a faire, amiable lady, limbes with an erring pencil, and drawes a libell, not a face, if he gives her not just features, and perfections: So in the translation of Bookes, he who makes a dull author elegant and quick; or a sharp, elegant author flat, rustick, rude and dull, by contrary wayes, commits the same sinne, and cannot be said to translate, but to transforme." That is sound sense, and judged by the high standard of Jasper Mayne, Francis Hickes has most valiantly acquitted himself.

He was the son of Richard Hickes, an arras weaver of Barcheston, in Warwickshire, and after taking the degree of Bachelor in the University of Oxford, which he entered in 1579, at the age of thirteen, he was diverted (says Thomas, his son) "by a country retirement;" henceforth he devoted his life to husbandry and Greek. Besides Lucian, he translated Thucydides and Herodian, the manuscripts of which are said to survive in the library of Christ Church. Possibly it was his long retirement that gave a turn of pedantry to his mind. It was but natural that in his remote garden he should exaggerate the importance of the knowledge acquired in patient solitude. But certain it is that the notes wherewith he decorated his margins are triumphs of inapposite erudition. When Lucian describes the famous cobwebs, each one of which was as big as an island of the Cyclades, Hickes thinks to throw light upon the text with this astonishing irrelevancy: "They are in the Ægean Sea, in number 13." The foible is harmless, nay pleasant, and consonant with the character of the learned recluse. Thus lived Francis Hickes, silent and unknown, until in 1630 he died at a kinsman's house at Sutton, in Gloucestershire. And you regret that his glory was merely posthumous. For, pedant as he was, he made known to his countrymen the Rabelais of the ancients, the veritable enemy of all the pedants, and matched a masterpiece of Greek with another masterpiece of sound and scholarly English.

LUCIAN

II

LUCIAN

II

BORN in Syria, educated, maybe, in Rome, a citizen of the great empire, familiar with the men and countries of the known world, Lucian remained until his death a devout Athenian. Though it pleased him to lecture through the length and breadth of Macedonia, though he carried culture to far-distant Gaul, he never forgot that—as a man of letters—he owed his allegiance to that miraculous city of the sea, which centuries ago had closed her book of glory. For to Lucian Athens was still an *alma mater*, who with splendour undimmed cherished the destinies of literature, and imposed her laws upon all the world. Never once does he hint at decline; never once does he suggest that the age of Pericles is past. With an admirable dogmatism he suppresses the intervening years, and pictures you a city which, still the home of Thucydides, listens awestruck to the wisdom of Socrates. The eminence of Rome avails not to turn him from his loyalty; though he never loses an occasion to quote a tag from the poets, though the lightest of his essays is embellished with a literary allusion, he knows naught of Virgil or Horace, and, what is still stranger, professes no acquaintance with Plautus or Terence. In brief, he chose his home and he chose his period, and there is little beyond a handful of references to prove that Rome had passed its Augustan age a hundred years before Lucian's birth, and that she was throughout his career the undisputed mistress of three continents.

He describes himself somewhere as one who lived with the ancients, and for all his ceaseless questing after new ideas, for all his valiant curiosity and research, for all his reckless destruction of idols, he was in literature as in life a staunch Conservative. His fancy wandered far back into the past, and that for which he had no appreciation was neither good nor bad: it was condemned to silence. History can hardly show a more violent paradox than this hard, sceptical, modern philosopher for whom nothing seemed real save the remote, and who, though a professed critic, had no word of praise or blame for the dominant literature of his time. He would conquer for his craft a whole kingdom of new material; but meanwhile he knew no other classics than Homer and Thucydides, than Herodotus and Æschylus. Sculpture for him meant the masterpieces of Phidias, of Polycletus, of Myron and Alcamenes, while Zeuxis and Apelles, the only painters worthy of admiration, might perchance be living yet. Wherefore it is not surprising that he wrote Greek with the austere suavity of the ancients. Though separated from his models by some five centuries, by as wide a lapse as divides Tennyson and Chaucer, he cultivated a style which Plato or Sophron would have understood, and he achieved this marvel without betraying the smallest trace of archaism. Could there be found a better example of tradition's tyranny? Lucian was a writer of delicate taste, to whom the extremes of affectation and artificiality were repugnant; yet so strong a hold had the Greek tongue kept upon the world, that his language would have appeared not only correct but admirable to the generation which heard Sophocles in the theatre of Dionysus. Imagine Mr. Pater apeing the style of Wycliffe and escaping notice! And Lucian's achievement is even stranger, for he was a foreigner dwelling in foreign cities, who chose Greek as Apuleius chose Latin, by a whimsical preference. Moreover, he never spoke it without an accent. "I talk Greek," he confesses himself, "like a barbarian"; but at least he wrote it like the Athenian he elected to be, and the mobs which listened to him could not detect the Syrian quality of his speech.

Nor was the Athens of his adoration the greedy, mean, unscrupulous city wherewith the Roman satirists have made us familiar. The hungry Greekling had no place in the paradise of lofty thought and noble conduct which Lucian saw in his dreams. The panegyric of Athens put into the mouth of Nigrinus, was obviously fashioned by his own brain, and could only befit a commonwealth of heroism and restraint. Yet its ardent sincerity is beyond question; and in

Lucian's eyes tradition still snatched the victory from decadence and death. Athens, then, is the proper refuge for the needy philosopher, who values the refinements of life above the indiscriminate scramble for wealth. For such a one, be he stranger or native-born, Athens has always a generous welcome. But luckless is he who would challenge her sympathy with ostentation, and capture her affection by display. Yet her citizens are moderate in their displeasure, and reproach even vulgarity with a jest. "The bath has enjoyed a long peace," they whisper to some foreigner who comes among them with an enormous retinue, "there is no need of a camp here." And when the upstart would astonish the town with a coat of many colours and purple trappings, "Look," they murmur, "the Spring is here already," or, "Where did this peacock spring from?" or, "Perhaps this robe is his mother's?" But for him who loves a simple life, and the pursuit of philosophy, Athens is the pleasantest resort, since there may you live in accordance with nature and in the presence of beautiful things. So Lucian contrasts Rome with this perfect harmony, and handsomely avenges the *Græculus esuriens.* "Why, poor devil, did you leave the sunlight?" asks Nigrinus of himself, when he sets foot in the capital of the Empire, where pleasure is admitted at every gate—pleasure with its attendant vice—and where all men race for the wealth which shall buy them gratification and satiety. There the slave of to-day is the rich man of to-morrow, and in the pitiless struggle honesty and learning are despised. How should philosophy prevail against the universal love of horse-racing? How should you expect simplicity from a city which sets up the statues of its jockeys at every street corner, and babbles only of its favourites' names? Thus Lucian, preferring the condemned, forgotten Athens, shows in his preference as in his style that he is the last of the Classics.

Yes, this Syrian with a provincial accent is a true classic—classic in the humane management of his style, classic also in his whole-hearted admiration of the past. But when you desert the form for the substance, you see how just is the commonplace, already quoted, that he was the first of the moderns. His achievement was nothing less than a miracle. He poured the new wine of modern experience into the old bottle of classic style, and neither wine nor bottle was spoilt. If taste and reverence restrained his expression, his thought was free as air, and with perfect truth he quoted the tag of Terence (doubtless from its Greek original): "Nothing that is human is foreign to me." Remembering also his familiarity with the Gods, to human he might have added divine. He found his material where he chose—in the shadowy palace of Olympus or in the highways of Rome. Now it was Zeus that engrossed his scorn, now it was Alexander the False Prophet that amused his fancy; and God or Charlatan was sufficient excuse for sly wit or swift imagination. But in nothing does he display the perfect freshness of his invention so evidently as in the bitter spirit of criticism which animates the most of his works. There is a legend that he left the sculptor's studio, where he should have learnt his art, because he broke in two the first block of marble submitted to his chisel. And this is a symbol of his career: his talent was analytic and destructive; he was always breaking superstition in pieces, or tearing the follies of mankind to shreds. Nor, when he had cleared the ground of its impeding rubble did he profess an ambition to build anew. He was of those happy ones who can live by the light of honesty and honour, and who need no compulsion of creed or system to drive them to virtue and content. Only he must examine all things; and, having discovered folly to himself, he must expose it to others for the satisfaction of his irony.

Thus he was the first critic not of literature merely, not of art, but of human life, and of all that it embraced. And if his ironic method of judgment was of his own devising, the shape of his criticism was fresh, various, imaginative. Now, his contempt would take the form of a tiny drama; now, he would half reveal his hidden meaning in a parable. But rarely does he descend to express a bald opinion in the bald terms of conviction. Of the dialogue he was the first and perfect master. Doubtless he had gathered hints from Plato and the mimes; doubtless he had learnt whatever the New Comedy had to teach of argument and repartee. And yet the dialogue, as he practised it, was essentially his own. His prose, more familiar than

Plato's, is as sprightly as the sprightliest comedy; and now for the first time was the ancient form, perfected in a sort of verse by Sophron, turned to the easy dissection of abuse, to the fierce confusion of the foolish and superstitious. He blends narrative with irony; he quickens a smile when his reprobation is heaviest; and to beguile the progress of his acid merriment he takes the reader on ship-board or by the pleasant lanes of Attica, or bids him look from the Acropolis on the shining city beneath.

And what were the terrors against which the critic hurled his satire? Like an excellent Conservative he hated the democrat who governs the assembly of the rich, who is hungry only for games, baths and spectacles, and who is ready in recompense for generosity to stone the wealthy citizen that feeds him. With a proper scorn he assailed the upstart who marks his accession to an ill-gotten fortune by adding two syllables to his name, the simple unnoticed Simon, who bids the world respect the dignity of Simonides. But he aimed his heaviest shafts at the philosophers, whose tangled beards and greasy mantles were his constant target. Now, the philosophers occupied in Lucian's world the space filled in after ages by the friars. Their gulching bellies refuted the plea of hunger and beggary. Though they would not work, still must they eat; and while they preached temperance to others, their noses were at once the symbol and the result of a too-patient devotion to the bottle. Eager only for money and advertisement, they believed their duty done when they had chosen a label, and put on the uniform of rags. Why do the Pythagoreans refuse to eat beans and flesh? Not for the sake of virtue, but that they may become famous by their very eccentricity, that they may be pointed at in the street with the murmured surprise: "There go the philosophers who abstain from flesh and beans."

So the philosophers pursued no calling; they performed no service to the State: a useless fardel of the earth, they shouted calumniously, and levied a pitiless blackmail on the rich and complacent. Yet, despite their constant habit of beggary, they pretended that they were high exalted above the need of money, and clamorously asserted that the wise man alone is rich. Though virtue was ever on their tongue, their heart was packed full of avarice and slander. A resolute training carried them safely through their studied performance, but the sight of an obol was sufficient to lead them astray, so that they resembled nothing so much as those monkeys whom a King of Egypt taught to perform the Pyrrhic dance, and whose performance was perfect, until one day a spectator threw a handful of nuts into the theatre. Instantly the well-trained rascals rid themselves of their masks, tore their coats to pieces, and scrambled for the nuts, remembering that if they were dancers afterwards they were monkeys first. So, too, the primal impulse of the man was too strong for the cant of the philosopher, and when (in *The Fisher*) the Cynic's wallet was open, they found therein—not a crust, a book, and a handful of beans—but gold, perfumes, a mirror, and a dice-box. In the miserable Peregrinus, however, all the sins of his class were met together, and Lucian, well skilled in the portraiture of the charlatan, never surpassed his contemptuous presentation of this impostor.

The illustrious Peregrinus then, who after the Zeus of Phidias was the single wonder of the earth, determined, by an act of sacrifice, not only to show his fellow citizens how a philosopher could die, but to illumine his name with a more brilliant advertisement than countless generations of Barnums have devised since. Having lived like Hercules, he determined like Hercules to die. Wherefore he built him a vast pyre at Olympia and died at the stake in the presence of thousands. Lucian, himself a witness of the philosopher's "roasting," describes how to the last Peregrinus, an ingrained coward, hoped that the crowd would frustrate his design. And bitter was his disappointment when, tired of the foolish spectacle, they cried aloud: "Make an end of it, make an end of it!" Thus died the foolish philosopher, who governed his life by vanity and the lust of popular approval. And Democritus would have laughed at the spectacle, and yet not found laughter enough, while "as for you," says Lucian to his friend Theagenes, "you laugh too, and above all, laugh when you hear others marvelling at such folly."

But if Lucian was unsparing in his contempt of vanity and pretence, he was generous in admiration of the true philosopher. He visited Nigrinus as a sick man visits a physician, and thereafter composed a sincere panegyric of his wisdom and eloquence. But the supreme hero, in his eyes, was Demonax, whose perfections he employs as a scourge wherewith to scourge the upstart and impostor, and whose praise is, in a sense, the severest criticism of his fellows. Above all he reveres this philosopher, because his wisdom had never made him forget that he was a gentleman as well as a scholar. He refused to vie with the footpads of Athens in eccentricity of garb and uncomeliness of person. He did nothing to attract the notice of the crowd; he dressed like others, and lived a life of distinguished simplicity. Above all he protected himself against the popular insolence by a bitterness of repartee, which, if it were not precisely the Socratic irony, was always touched with Attic grace. And as Lucian admired the few wise men who found wisdom elsewhere than in the blind adherence to a school, so for Philosophy, his dear mistress, he cherished an undying reverence. But alas! it was in vain that he sought her. "I know not where she lives," he wrote, "and yet I have wandered up and down a weary while seeking her house that I might pay her a visit."

Possibly he never found her save in a dream, yet sedulously did he practise the rites of her worship, and the bitterest of his irony is devoted to her defence. But of literature also he was an eager champion, and a theory of criticism may be deduced from his casual utterances. He followed Aristotle implicitly in the belief that the end and aim of art was to give pleasure.

He shrank from realism as he shrank from novelty, as he shrank from every ingenuity which marred the perfect beauty of a piece. There is a certain pathos in the apology which he made, at the top of his fame, for his favourite dialogue. An over zealous friend had proclaimed him the "Prometheus of literature," and he disowns the name in a passage of admirable dignity. "Perhaps," says he, in effect, "I am called Prometheus because my works are fresh in form and follow the example of no man. . . . . But in my eyes strangeness without beauty has no merit . . . . and I should deserve to be torn to pieces by sixteen vultures if I thought that a work of art could be distinguished by novelty alone." So he would prove that the form is no new thing at all, but the legitimate child of Dialogue and Comedy; so he would reject the false praise which his admirers would bid him share with the black camel of Bactria or with the striped man that Ptolemy brought to Egypt. So in the *Zeuxis*, this ancient classic, who could not withhold his hand from new material, and who always had ready a new form of parable, adds to his eloquent denunciation of novelty a candid defence of technique against the tyranny of subject. He had left a lecture-room, he tells you, furious with the ill-considered applause of his audience, and especially enraged against the constant compliment heaped upon the novelty of his discourse.*

* The shouts of the people were as fatuous then as to-day. Ω τῆς καινότητος, they cried; Ἡράκλεις, τῆς παραδοξολογίας. εὐμήχανος ἄνθρωπος. οὐδὲν ἄν τις εἴποι τῆς ἐπινοίας νεαρώτερον.

As he went homeward, chagrined that he is admired only because he has left the common road; that he receives the praise of a facile conjurer; that the harmony of his Attic style, the swiftness of his imagination, his many-coloured fancy count for nothing; he bethought him of the mishap which befel Zeuxis. Now, Zeuxis painted a family of centaurs, the mare stretched upon the deep grass, and the centaur keeping watch in the background, a long-haired, savage child of the mountain. But the people passed by in idle contempt not only the beauty of the drawing and the exquisite harmony of the colour, but also the variety of expression, and the changing characters of the centaurs. They only applauded the singular motive, because they had never seen it treated before. "Roll up the canvas," said Zeuxis to his pupil, "and take it home. These men only praise the mud of our art. In their eyes the novelty of a subject eclipses every excellence of execution."

The rebuke is commonplace to-day, though it has seldom been administered with a better tact. But in Lucian's time it was as strange as the craze of invention which he condemned, and despite his own protest he must once again be flattered for his originality. Nor was his contempt of realism less apt than his hatred of charlatanry, and to illustrate his dislike he chose the art he loved the best, the art of pantomime. Moreover, after his wont, he put his criticism in the form of an anecdote. "Once upon a time there was a mime who played the part of Ajax mad, and he played it with so reckless a disregard of the rules of his art that he did not represent madness; he seemed rather to be mad himself. He tore the coat from the back of one of those who beat time with their iron sandals, and snatching a flute from one of the players, he struck Ulysses, who stood by exulting in his victory, so fiercely on the head that he surely would have died had not his helmet broken the force of the blow. And then the whole theatre went mad with Ajax; the spectators leapt to their feet, they shouted, they tore off their cloaks. The more foolish among them, unable to distingush between good and evil, thought they saw before them a lifelike representation of madness, while the more intelligent, ashamed at what was going on, were reluctant to condemn the performance by their silence, and attempted by applause to cover the folly of the performance. But all the while they knew that it was the madness not of Ajax but of the player that they were witnessing. The poor devil, still unsatisfied, went to yet greater lengths. He descended into the theatre and took his seat between two of consular rank, each of whom feared that he would seize and flog him like a sheep. And some wondered and some laughed, and others were afraid that the actor's feigned madness would turn to a true malady."

Never were the limits of art expressed in an apter parable. How well we know the foolish man who shouts "lifelike" when he contemplates an outrage upon good taste! And the conclusion is as wise as the parable. Imitation, says Lucian, is not reality;

and he who would actually perform that which he should represent is no artist, but a madman. Even the actor, relates the critic, was so ashamed at this triumph of excess that he never again played the part of Ajax, though it had been written for him. "It is enough," he murmured, "to have been mad once," and straightway with a reasonable generosity, unique in the annals of the stage, he resigned his part to a popular rival, who played the mad scene with perfect restraint, and received the highest possible praise for that he never overstepped the legitimate boundaries of his art.

Simple as is the anecdote, it expresses a judgment of perennial sanity. What else is the realist than the actor who mistakes the madness of Ajax for his own, and who would willingly break the head of his neighbour and assault the people, if only he may be certain of an instant and violent effect? Indeed, as you turn over the pages of Lucian, you understand that he was not only modern, but prophetic. He anticipated by many centuries the steam-engine and the telegraph. Timolaus (in *The Ship*) would announce the name of the Olympian victor in Babylon the very day the race was run; he would breakfast in Syria, and dine in Italy. And yet more wonderful, Lucian provides in his criticism for the last-born vice or virtue of literature. He is always ready to ridicule our folly with a quip, and to turn the flash of his irony upon a modern ineptitude. But perhaps he nowhere shows himself a truer prophet than in his admirable essay upon

Pantomime. This essay, inspired by the unmeasured enthusiasm of the poet, and tempered with the genial pedantry of the scholar, is the perfection of ironic criticism. As you read it you think perforce of Deburau, of Nodier, of the *Funambules*, with its sawdust and oranges. You might be reading a transfigured rhapsody devised by Gautier himself, or looking upon a brilliant picture of which Janin's *Théâtre à Quatre Sous* is a pallid reflection. For here is the real essence of romantic pantomime as it was praised in Athens by the wisest of philosophers, and adored on the Boulevard du Temple by the wittiest of critics.

So pantomime in Lucian's eyes is the greatest of the arts. While he follows the opinion of Aristotle, he embroiders it with so extravagant a bravery that the austere author of *The Poetics* would never recognise his own. As it is the finest, so it is the oldest of the arts. The earliest dancers* were the stars, and even the planets wove a stately, rhythmical measure. And then with a sly parade of inapposite history, Lucian reviews the progress of the art in all ages and countries, from the savagery of the Corybantes and the finer elegance of Neoptolemus, the son of Achilles, to the practice of his own day. He finds it superior to tragedy, in that, while it employs the same materials, it combines them with a far greater freedom and variety. Thus, still true to his noble enthusiasm, he sketches the mime, and demands of him so vast a learning and

* Ὄρχησις is Lucian's Greek for pantomime, an art indistinguishable from the dance.

prowess, that you wonder that he was ever able to gratify his legitimate taste. The mime (or dancer), says he, must win the favour of Mnemosyne and Polymnia. Like Homer's Calchas, he must know the present, past, and future. As it is his function to imitate, to give an outward expression of thought, to make clear the obscure, his highest praise is that which Thucydides found for Pericles, that he knew what he should and could explain it. Moreover, since the material of pantomime is ancient history, the mime must be familiar with all things from Chaos to Cleopatra, and even with this mastery of universal learning he is at the threshold of his art. Dumb, he must be understood, and though he speak not, yet men must hear him.

His perfection is measured in the rebuke administered to Demetrius the Cynic, who thought so ill of pantomime that he charged the mime with relying for his effect upon trivial accessories—the trappings of silk, the dainty mask, the music of the flute. Whereupon a most renowned actor, who best knew the history of his art, and excelled all living men in the beauty of his gesture, freed his stage for the moment of all decoration. He put aside both costume and mask; he silenced the music, suppressed the chorus and performed alone the Love of Ares and Aphrodite. Without aid he represented the betrayal of the intrigue, the trap laid by Hephaestus, the shame of Aphrodite, the fearful supplication of Ares; and with so exquisite a precision that Demetrius made immediate submission.

He put no limit on the extravagance of his praise. "I hear," said he to the actor, "all that you do; I do not merely see; in truth you appear to speak with your fingers."

In such terms was Deburau praised by a hundred critics who knew not Lucian, and the universality of the criticism is evidence, maybe, of its truth. But Lucian has not yet exhausted the qualities of his actor; for he would have him know as much of life as of history. He must not stay like a limpet on his rock; he must know the manners of many cities, and travel the wide world up and down. Grace, especially grace of hand, is essential; strength, also, must belong to the perfect mime. And then having united in his proper person all the elegances and harmonious gestures, having mastered history and science and studied the intelligence of mankind, he still falls short of his art if he do not compel the spectators to see in his performance their own passions and experience as in a mirror. In brief, avoiding the very appearance of realism, he must suggest by a movement of hand or eye the poignant moment of a tragedy or the heart-whole laughter of a trivial farce. 'Tis a pleasing paradox, this elevation of what to-day is wrongly held the humblest of the arts to the throne of dignity. Yet Lucian is justified even in his paradox. The other arts, says he, express one emotion; pantomime presents them all. It shows you body and soul inextricably blended; it combines the form of sculpture, the colour of painting with the swift movement of life and of the brain. And you imagine this ancient philosopher, with a smile for the pedantic irony of his own treatise, sitting day after day at his favourite spectacle, and administering to Crates the same reproof which Gautier might have framed for them who detected at the *Funambules* nothing but sawdust and grotesquery.

Thus, while in his creative work Lucian remained a critic, his criticism was always creative. Yet now and again he laid aside his more serious intent, and drew a portrait for its own sake. His *Alexander, or the False Prophet*, is a masterpiece of ruffianism; and though he confesses that he bit the impostor's hand when he should have kissed it, it is evident that he delighted in his villainous adroitness, in the splendour of his purple and gold, in the pitiful trick of the tamed and harmless snake. *The Dialogues of Courtesans*, again, had fulfilled their admirable purpose the instant they were written. The type, with its small jealousies, its worldly wisdom, its half-assumed timidity has never been more skilfully realised; while the mother, fat, careful, of no age, and blousy (you are sure) displays the same eternal, unchanging qualities in Lucian's delicate prose as in the pictured satire of Forain. So the erudite philosopher kept his sleepless eye upon life, and, for all his learning, turned whatever was serious into merriment. Not even did he spare the gout, which, says rumour, carried him off at last. For he immortalised the universal enemy in an admirable burlesque, whose wit should have procured him a grateful release from pain. But doubtless he despised the plague, and died, as he lived, a satirist, free and frank, without wish or regret, with no other ambition than to laugh at those who desire the unattainable, and yet respect philosophy.

SIR THOMAS URQUHART

SIR THOMAS URQUHART

FROM whichever point you approach Cromarty, you seem to have arrived at the world's end. You may drive across the Black Isle, or you may enter the land-locked harbour in a casual ferry-boat. But you can go no further, for there are the Suters to bar your progress, and there is the narrow street leading nowhither to remind you that at least one county town is remote from the populous highway. Its aspect is ancient, cold and grey, and yet the enlarging sea has compelled the new town again and again to supersede the old, so that it is less time than a forgotten fashion which gives the impression of immemorial solidity. The houses are trim ; trim too are the gardens ; and withal marked by that austerity which should defend them for ever from the reproach of villadom. An alley, dignified with the name of the Vennel, carries the traveller far back into the past, while the dark aspect of the fisherfolk, more gipsy than highlander, proves that Cromarty is still a fastness. It is no surprise to detect over the red lintel of a dilapidated stable the scutcheon of those brave men who once were hereditary sheriffs of the place ; you marvel only at the intermittent golf-club, which declares that no corner is free from the national scourge ; you only regret that the sentiment of Hugh Miller should eclipse the glory of Sir Thomas Urquhart. But neither Hugh Miller nor golf can cheapen Cromarty nor persuade her to increase her borders. For north and south the Suters stretch seawards, this one bleak and low-lying, that one lofty with its coronal of trees, and rich in the mysteries of Witches' Hole and Gallows' Hill, and either resolute to oppose encroachment. From the land they are a barrier against the mastery of the sea ; from the sea they appear sentinels of refuge—Σώτηρες, so Sir Thomas called them—which should point the path of safety to the sailor in distress.

Such is Cromarty, which boasts to have given birth, in 1605, to Sir Thomas Urquhart, most fantastical of Scotsmen. His ancestors had been hereditary sheriffs and proprietors of the soil for twenty-two hundred years and more, if we may trust his fearless imagination. And these centuries are but a fringe upon his antiquity. So noble a conceit had he in the house of Cromarty, that he traced his genealogy through all ages and all countries to Adam himself. There are no great cities, and few great families, which did not aid in the making of Sir Thomas Urquhart, and all are set forth with pride and circumstance in the Παντοχρονοχανον, *or a Peculiar Promptuary of Time*. The effrontery of this ingenious piece is no less enchanting than its simple faith. The author twists folk-lore into fact, and bombasts his quick invention with all the circumstance of historical research. Doubtless he compiled his descent in emulation of Pantagruel, but while Rabelais laughed at his own pompous imagination, Sir Thomas was eager to believe the wildest fiction, and to forget that he had not written authority for every vain extravagance.

Thus Adam, the common father of us all, "surnamed the Protoplast," was created out of the red earth, merely that he might be the forbear of all the Urquharts. Better still, the sixteenth in descent from the renowned Protoplast, one Esormon, son of Pasiteles, was surnamed **οὐροχάρτος** for his fortune in the wars and his affable conversation, and so gave his name to the illustrious family whose glory culminated in Sir Thomas Free of Speech. Now Esormon, albeit he was born in the year before Christ two thousand one hundred and thirty-nine, was Prince of Achaia, and had for his arms "three banners, three ships and three ladies, in a field *dor*, with a picture of a young lady above the waste, holding in her right hand a brandished sword, and a branch of myrtle in the left, for crest; and for supporters two Javanites after the souldier-habit of Achaia." Thus heraldry flourished in the childhood of the world, and it is no surprise that Molin, the fortieth from Adam, married Panthea, Deucalion's daughter, and allied the Urquharts with one of the best families in Greece. A century later

Propetes took to wife Hypermnestra, "the choicest of Danaus' fifty daughters," while a less remote ancestor espoused the Queen of Sheba, that no talent should be lacking to the perfected Sir Thomas.

Some thousand years before Christ you touch Scottish soil, for when Alypos, the Queen of Sheba's own son, married Proteusa, the sister of Eborak, who founded York, Scotland was already called Olbion (or Albion in the Aeolick dialect), already the castle of Edinburgh frowned upon the valley where Prince's Street was presently to be built, and the promontories of Cromarty had won the name of Σώτηρες, which they retain unto this day. But the Urquharts had not yet come into their own. True, Alypos had paid a casual visit to the harbour of Ochonchar, now called Cromarty, and Beltistos, the seventy-sixth in descent from Adam, had founded the castle of Urquhart above Inverness. But it was reserved for the honoured Nomostor to build that house upon the South Suter which remained for two thousand years the home of the Urquharts. Henceforth these heroes remained within their own borders, fighting the Picts, and making plain their eloquence to all the world. Neither Lutork, the valiant conqueror of Lochaber, not the famous Stichopaeo himself, neither Sosomenos nor Eunoemon, husband of the first Morray that ever came to Scotland, strayed beyond the limits of Cromarty and its fortress. So with Sir Jasper, who had the dexterity to cure the King's Evil, and who still flourished when William the Norman invaded England, we emerge from fable into the semblance of history, and hear with a mild surprise that Thomas, born 1476, was surnamed Paterhemon because "he had of his wife Helen Abenethie, a daughter of my Lord Salton, five-and-twenty sons, all men, and eleven daughters, all married women." Far more puzzling is the nickname of Walter, Sir Thomas's own great-grandfather. For he was called "Exaftallocrinus," for no better reason than that he judged others by himself. But there were learned men in ancient Cromarty, and instantly the real Sir Thomas was called to the throne the popular voice acclaimed him Parresiastes, or Free of Speech, after the same Greek work which, says Rabelais, gave to the Parisians their name and title.

With such a pedigree it was plainly impossible to remain obscure, and Thomas Urquhart gave early signs of the scholarship and fancy which ever distinguished him. After a boyhood spent in the castle, which then stood upon the southern Suter, and devoted doubtless to the zealous discovery of family secrets, he passed to the University of Aberdeen, for which he retained a ceaseless respect and admiration. His loyalty bade him spare no occasion of praising those who, like himself, owed their education to Aberdeen, which, said he, "for honesty, good fashions and learning, surpasseth as far all other towns and cities in Scotland, as London doth for greatness, wealth, and magnificence, the smallest hamlet or village in England."

And so, his head packed with all the knowledge

of his time, and his quick hand always at his sword-hilt, he set forth upon the conquest of Europe. In this enterprise he followed the fashion of his age and country. When Urquhart went upon his travels the whole world was the heritage of Scotland. There was no University that did not seek its professors from the savage country beyond the Tweed, and wherever the rumour of war was heard, there were a a hundred Scots ready to sell their sword and their life in the service of the foreigner. While Sinclair taught mathematics at Paris, Seaton took his degrees at Padua, and disported his "lofty and bravashing humour" at Rome; Dempster travelled the whole length of France and Italy, teaching the humanities, and resenting with his right arm the smallest affront put upon his dignity. And before all, Crichton, the glorious and invincible Crichton, had carried away the palm, whether for scholarship or valour, in every capital in Europe. It was in emulation, then, of such heroes as these that Thomas Urquhart left his native Cromarty, convinced that no learning was too high for his attainment, no enemy too strong for his assault. Wherever he went, he bore himself as a gallant gentleman, adding to the rare store of his learning, and winning golden opinions for his courage and address. If he had only composed a history of his wanderings instead of attempting to square the circle, how rich had been the record! As it is, we must be content with his few digressions, and piece together a slender biography from a handful of casual hints.

He made a "peragration" (so he calls it) of France, Spain and Italy, whence he crossed to Sicily, and was most astonished to discover at Messina a man who posed for the Great Alexander of Macedon. Ever anxious, despite the weight of his immense learning, to recall what was trivial or eccentric, he tells you no more of Madrid than that he there saw "a bald-pated fellow who believed he was Julius Cæsar, and therefore went constantly in the street with a laurel-crown on his head." His mastery of languages was perfect; he spoke all tongues "with the liveliness of the country accent," and there was no city whereof he might not have passed for a native, had not his patriotism rejected the imposture. Did a Spaniard or a Frenchman suggest the disguise, "he plainly told them, without any bones, that truly he had as much honour by his own country." For in those days, he boasted, "the name of a Scot was honourable over all the world, and the glory of his ancestors was a passport and safe conduct sufficient for any traveller." Nor did Urquhart do aught to besmirch this fair fame. He was as prompt in a quarrel as in the exercise of his tongue, and in the early years, before his brains "were ripened for eminent undertakings," he thrice entered the lists to vindicate his native land from calumnies. And thrice he disarmed his antagonist, compelling him at the price of his life to acknowledge his error, so that, "in lieu of three enemies that formerly they were, I acquired three constant friends, both to myself and my compatriots." Thus he wandered over the world, obeying the valiance of his heart, and yet packing his head with all the jumbled and intricate sciences, unrivalled in swordsmanship, and always alert in the fashionable art of disputation. But so strenuous a patriot could not spend his life in foreign service, and Urquhart was still young when he returned a finished courtier to his father's house in Cromarty.

He brought with him a library which he valued beyond all else, especially because it did not contain three books, "which were not of his own purchase, and all of them together, in the order wherein he had ranked them, compiled like to a compleat nosegay of flowers, which in his travels he had gathered out of the gardens of above sixteen several kingdoms." In Cromarty, indeed, he had no resource but study. A courtier and a scholar, he felt as little sympathy with field sports as with the barbarous life of his fellows. While others were pleased in the dead season of winter to search for wild fowl, wading through many waters, he would stay at home, employed in diversions of another nature, "such as optical secrets, mysteries of natural philosophy, reasons for the variety of colours, the finding out of the longitude, and the squaring of the circle." And when he was twitted for his inaction by those who esteemed bodily exercise above the recreation of the mind, he had the satisfaction of supping excellently, while the sportsmen were too weary to touch the birds which had fallen to their guns. So, in the seclusion of his castle, this descendant of Danaus became the master pedant of his time. Not only was he familiar with all the extravagant learning of Europe, but he was already busied in the composition of those unnumbered treatises whose loss after Worcester fight he lamented until his death.

Alas! an end soon came to the repose which is necessary for the squaring of the circle or the discovery of a universal language. The house of Urquhart fell upon ruin. The old Sir Thomas, in spite of the oath given to Alexander, Lord Elphinstone, on his marriage, that he would hand on his estate unencumbered, became the sudden prey of creditors. The reason of this disaster is uncertain; but it was rather amiable carelessness than wanton extravagance which undid the generous and worthy knight. He had given to all who asked with thoughtless prodigality; he had never refused to be surety for any; yet herein his kindness was matched by good fortune, and he did not "pay above two hundred pounds English for all his vadimonial favors." However, his creditors at last began to clamour. With a recklessness which you can easily understand in the father of his son, he had neglected his household and forgotten his tradesmen. Unfaithful servants had filched much of his personal estate; swindling bailiffs had embezzled his rents; and by the frequency of disadvantageous bargains in which the slyness of the subtle merchant involved him, his loss came unawares upon him, and irresistibly, like an armed man. The mishap was the stranger because in the arbitrament of another's affairs none was held so wise as Sir Thomas Urquhart ; yet, said his son, he thought it "derogating to the nobility of his house to look too closely into his own purse."

The result was ruin, and in 1637 the hereditary Sheriff of Cromarty was so hard pressed that he was forced to seek relief from the King. The relief was granted in a letter of protection from Charles I., which defended him "from all diligence at the instance of his creditors." But, in the meantime, his sons had taken what steps they might to secure the remains of their inheritance ; and despite their protestations of filial obedience, had seized upon their father, and imprisoned him in an upper chamber of his own castle, called "the inner dortour." Whether they resorted to this savagery, that the old knight might be prevented from the conclusion of a bad bargain, or whether they were impelled by disappointment and revenge, remains unknown ; but true it is that they kept their father locked up the best part of a week, and that they only escaped the proper consequence of their cruelty by the interposition of the Privy Council. And notwithstanding this interlude of enmity, the son never tired of praising the justice, honour, and munificence of the father. And you like to think that his solitary fault was inspired by a stern fidelity to the interests of his house.

Henceforth misfortune was his constant bedfellow.

Not only was the estate encumbered beyond hope of redress, but Urquhart, a staunch Episcopalian, stood for the King, and hated the Covenant with all the fury of a travelled gentleman and a pleasure-loving courtier. Moreover, he was neither sufficiently cunning to dissemble his opinion, nor sufficiently dishonest to espouse an infamous cause for his own profit. He found upon his own country the three foul blots of tergiversation, covetousness and hypocrisy; and he exposed the blots with all the eloquence and iteration at his command. Scotland, said he, was ruined by the selfishness of Kirks and Presbyteries. The minister was always the greediest man in the parish, the most unwilling to bestow anything in deeds of charity. He denounced without ceasing the democratical tyranny of the Kirk, and with all the Cavalier's eagerness to back his opinion with the sword, he forcibly opposed Lord Fraser and his allies. A retainer of his house was the first to lose his life in conflict with the bloody Covenanters; and Urquhart, having marched upon Aberdeen, was circumvented by the Earl Marischal after a brief success, and compelled to embark in the presence of six hundred enemies for Berwick-on-Tweed. Henceforth he was exiled to the English court; two years later—in 1641—he was knighted by the King at Whitehall, and the following year by the death of his father he inherited a worthless estate, and with the Sheriffdom of Cromarty a yet more worthless title.

Poor and unfriended, he despised conciliation.

He whose tongue had known no mercy found no mercy in the hearts of his enemies. His father left him but a poor six hundred a year, and for encumbrances twelve or thirteen thousand pounds of debt, "five brethren, all men, and two sisters almost marriageable," with as fine a set of importunate creditors as ever disturbed a scholar's peace. All attempts at a settlement were frustrated by the malice and envy of merchants and money-lenders, and at the last Urquhart had no resource but contempt and vituperation. How, indeed, should this arrogant gentleman, this marvel of the perfections, grant satisfaction to the greed of scoundrels? The fiercest of his creditors was one Leslie of Findrassie, whose name he protests he will never mention, but whose name is rarely off his tongue. This rascal, who kept "his daughters the longer unhusbanded that they might serve him for so many stalking-horses, whereby to intangle some neighbourhood woodcocks," pursued the Lord of Cromarty with an ingenuity of venom. Not only did he decline to treat with his enemy upon any terms, but he attacked one of his victim's farms with all the horse and foot he could command. He even attempted to quarter a troop upon Sir Thomas, that he might the more quickly bring him to surrender. Worse than all, he contrived the seizure of his library, and the destruction of not a few manuscripts which their author held priceless. But fruitlessly did Urquhart bewail that the wickedest of the land should be permitted to possess his inheritance; fruitlessly did he deplore the sacrilege of those who dismantled the honour of a house and dilapidated an ancient estate. Time was, said he, when no stranger might own an ell of Scottish land, when even Rizzio was not permitted to purchase a hundred pounds of rent whereby to acquire a title. But now the structure of ancient grandeur was "crumbled into the very rubbish of a neophytick parity." So his own land was sequestrated, and if after his father's death he pursued his studies at Cromarty, he lived rather as a prisoner than as a sheriff, and the utmost of his freedom was to hold all things ready for a siege.

While his creditors were inexorable, the Kirk, which had many an ancient offence to avenge, did not lag behind in evil-doing. At the outset his inherited right of patronage was curtailed, and, that he might be the more heavily embarrassed, the single parish, which contained the churches of Cullicudden and Kirkmichael, was divided into two, and the miserable Urquhart compelled to provide the double stipend. His protest was as vain as his indignation. To fight the Kirk was to kick against the pricks, and this intrepid warrior would never withdraw an unprotected foot. His arguments in his own behalf were convincing enough to ensure failure, and yet Sir Thomas was not of those who would veil the truth for a present advantage. No, he boldly proclaimed himself *Christianus Presbyteromastix*, and went unflinching to his doom. For the Kirk and State, not content with stripping him of his goods, carried their hostility still further, and in 1649 had declared him rebel and traitor.

But Urquhart, like Joseph II., was *royaliste de son métier*, and, though he regretted his bitter spoliation, he cared not that the world called him rebel. He threw himself with the greater fury into the fray, he fought the last fight for his rightful King, and he suffered at Worcester the culmination of his disasters. For not only was Worcester the one battle wherein he gave ground to the enemy, but in the kennels of Worcester City he lost the precious manuscripts which were to have conferred immortality upon him. To this ultimate mishap he recurs and recurs, though he nowhere explains why he should have gone into battle with the work of a lifetime at his back. However, no sooner was the fight finished, than the victorious soldiers broke into Master Spilsbury's house ("a very honest man, and hath an exceeding good woman to his wife"), and there found three portmantles full of very precious commodity, or in other words of manuscripts in folio. These inestimable treasures were presently devoted to the packing up of "figs, dates, almonds, caraway, and other such like dry confections," to the kindling of tobacco pipes, or even to worse employments. A few fragments alone were saved, from which Sir Thomas was able to rescue such treatises as remain. But with the defeat of Worcester his active life was finished. What could he, "a Scot and a prisoner of war," make or mar in the London of the Roundheads?

Cromwell, in truth, treated him with more than common liberality, permitting him to print his elaborate vindication, setting him free upon parole, and "enlarging him to the extent of the lines of London's communication." For all these courtesies he is properly thankful, and he closes the epilogue of all his works with a eulogy of Mr. Roger Williams. By what freak of destiny the reverend preacher of Providence in New England should have come to Urquhart's aid is left unexplained, but certain it is that this monument of piety not only presented Urquhart with "many worthy books set forth by him," but frequently solicited the Parliament and Council of State in his behalf. In brief, writes Sir Thomas, "he did approve himself a man of such discretion and inimitably sanctified parts, that an archangel from Heaven could not have shown more goodness with less ostentation!" But Mr. Roger Williams solicited in vain, and the victim himself had no better luck. His desperate appeals to Cromwell for the restoration of his estates and for his unconditioned liberty failed. Nor was there from the first a chance of success. He could not cloak his loyalty to the Stuarts, even when he addressed the Lord Protector; and so, having committed to the press some scraps and shreds of his dispersed masterpieces, he escaped the vigilance of his warders, set sail for France, the country he loved so well, and never again set foot in Scotland. His whimsical death well suited so whimsical a life. He died of laughter, saith rumour, on hearing that Charles II. was restored to his kingdom. And thus, by a last misfortune, his persistent loyalty availed him nothing, since, at the very moment of victory, his sense of incongruity carried him beyond the hope of gratitude or reward. Others inherited the estate of which he was so worthily proud, and even in Cromarty itself Urquhart was soon the shadow of a name.

Despite the devastation of Worcester, Sir Thomas was able in the two years which followed the battle to prove himself not only the greatest translator of all time, but the master of as fantastic a style as ever came to the aid of an eccentric imagination. He was not new to authorship: as early as 1641, the year of his knighthood, he had dedicated a volume of *Epigrams* to the Marquis of Hamilton. But this slender volume gives not the slightest promise of talent. The sestets, which fill the greater part of the book, are indistinguished and indistinguishable. There is no reason why any one should have written them. On the other hand, there is no reason why any one should have not. They express the usual commonplaces: the inevitableness of death and the worth of endeavour. A mildly Horatian sentiment is dressed up in the tattered rags of Shakespeareanism; and the surprise is that the author, whose prose is restrained by no consideration of sound or sense, should deem it worth while to print so tame a collection of exercises. His real epigrams, however, are still in manuscript, and are not likely to get into print. They number, it is said, some eleven hundred, "contryved, clerked, and digested . . . in a thirteen weeks' time," thus arguing in the author "a great maturity and promptnesse of wit."*

Four years later came *The Trissotretras: or a Most Exquisite Table for resolving all manner of Triangles*, in which the greatness of Urquhart is already foreshadowed. This work, "published for the benefit of those that are mathematically affected," is reputed unintelligible even to professors of mathematics, but it is prefaced by a dedication "to my deare and loving mother," and a eulogy of that "brave spark" Lord Napier of Merchiston, which are composed in the true vein. However, it was not until defeat had stimulated invention that Urquhart came into the full and free possession of his amazing style. The 'Εκσκυβαλαυρον, *or the Discovery of a most exquisite Jewel*, and the *Logopandecteision, or an Introduction to the Universal Language*, have not their counterpart in any literature. Though the one serves "to frontal a vindication of the honour of Scotland," though the other was contrived "for the utilitie of all pregnant and ingenious spirits," the glorification of Sir Thomas Urquhart is the object of both.

* In 1683 this manuscript belonged to George Ogilvie, Master of Banff, and afterwards, according to Dr. Irving, who was fortunate enough to see it, it passed into the possession of Lord Hyndford. It was then sold for £23 10s., and became the property of James Gibson Craig. Some time since it figured, for the modest sum of £10 10s., in the catalogue of an Edinburgh bookseller.

The author discusses history and theology, philosophy and politics; yet all the sciences are but a cloak to his own excellences. Sir Thomas Urquhart is a captive; the world stands idle upon its axis, the sun declines to rise and set; liberate Sir Thomas, and the universe will resume its functions; darkness will usurp the light at the proper season, and the brilliance of day will succeed to the sullen obscurity of night. But in one respect his modesty conquered his ambition of notoriety, and he pretends to keep the secret of authorship inviolate. The 'Εκσκυβαλαυρον is written with the definite aim of eulogising Scotland and of restoring the great and good Sir Thomas to his own kingdom. And who wrote it? From internal evidence it is plainly disinterested—for Sir Thomas is ever belauded in the third person. Just as the famous pedigree, that illustrious Παντοχρονοχανον which gives the Knight of Cromarty Deucalion for an ancestor, was rescued from the battlefield by "a surprising honest and civil officer of Colonel Pride's regiment," and prefaced by an unknown and mysterious G. P., so the vindication of Scotland and Sir Thomas might have been composed by a partial stranger. The object is frankly confessed: "He is the only man for whom this book is intended, the mere scope whereof is the furtherance of his weal and the credit of his country." Again, he describes himself as "the author whose muse I honour, and the strains of whose pen to imitate is my greatest ambition." And then, weary of mystification he boasts with an engaging frankness "that it mentioneth Sir Thomas Urquhart in the third person, which seldom is done by any author in a treatise of his own penning!"

But in truth it was his constant fancy to cover reality with a shield of romance, and to defend his purpose with perpetual digression. And thus, having designed a lofty panegyric of himself and his country, he breaks off—in the *Exquisite Jewel*—into a brief description of his Universal Language. But he reveals no more than shall whet the public appetite, since he desires to sell his invention for the wealth and leisure which should justly be his. The secret of learning which he claims to have discovered will, says he, abridge the labour of scholars by two years out of five, a benefit which cannot be estimated at less than ten thousand pounds a year. Nor does he make appeal to the generosity of Parliament. If only the Lord Protector will restore to him the inheritance which the "cochlimatory wasps" of the Presbytery have torn from him, he is ready to devote his whole life to the cause of learning, and to the manifest embellishment of the Scottish nation. But the Lord Protector was not tempted to interfere, and Sir Thomas's Language remains a vague and summary sketch.

The praise of Scotland, on the other hand, is neither summary nor vague. No literature in the world can show a nobler piece of boastfulness, and, despite its elaborate decoration, it is an historical treatise of enduring value. Now, Sir Thomas had witnessed the supremacy of his countrymen both in the schools and in the tourney. He had seen the discomfiture of their opponents in all the capitals of Europe, and himself had carried off a dozen trophies. None, then, was better qualified to sing the praise of the ever-renowned Bothwell, or to applaud the prowess of Francis Sinclair, the valiant bastard of Caithness, who conquered a gallant nobleman of High Germany in the presence of the Emperor and all his Court. But the supreme hero of all time in Urquhart's eye was Crichton, *Scotus Admirabilis*, the matchless and noble-hearted warrior, the irresistible lover, the miracle of eloquence. If Sir Thomas failed to force his Universal Language upon the world's acceptance, he invented that which was far more wonderful: the Admirable Crichton. A single episode, dropped by hazard into the *Exquisite Jewel*, not only conferred legitimate glory upon a renowned adventurer, but fixed for all time the type ot perfection. His achievement at the Duke of Mantua's Court; the glorious victory of wit snatched from the thrice-renowned University of Paris; his brilliant appearance at the Louvre in a buff suit, "more like a favourite of Mars, than one of the Muses' minions, where, in presence of some princess of the Court, and great ladies that came to behold his gallantry, he carried away the ring fifteen times on end, and broke as many lances as the Saracen"—these are related in a very gust of enthusiasm, and with a breathless torrent of strange and lofty words. And, then, to prove that bombast was not the only note upon his lyre, he describes with a veritable pathos the death of Crichton at the hands of the prince whose court he had purged of a monster. The amplitude of his vocabulary merely quickens the narrative and intensifies the emotion. When Crichton falls, you can but echo the frenzied threnody of the princess, who, "rending her garments and tearing her hair, like one of the Graces possessed with a Fury, spoke thus: 'O villains! what have you done? you vipers of men, that have thus basely slain the valiant Crichton, the sword of his own sex, and the buckler of ours, the glory of this age, and restorer of the lost honour of the Court of Mantua: O Crichton, Crichton!'"

Having thus chanted the excellences of Scotland, he descends, in the *Logopandecteision*, to a nearer consideration of the Universal Language. Yet again his pedantry holds him but a moment, and he is soon inspired to an elaborate iteration of his grievances. Never was a grammatical treatise set forth with a more whimsical parade of titles. True, the first book, styled *Neaudethaumata*, is concerned with the wonders of the new speech, which with its four numbers and eleven genders is to find one word, and one only, for each idea, and to teach by words "in the matter of colours the proportion of light, shadow or darkness commixed in them." But he soon leaves the meaner theme of science; and so far is he from grammar in his second book, that it is intituled *Chrestasebeia, or Impious Dealing of Creditors*, and thus you are easily prepared to consider the *Cleronomaporia, or the Intricacy of a Distressed Successor, or Apparent Heir.* Once again he describes the innumerable benefits he has conferred, or is willing to confer, upon mankind ; once more with the honestest indiscretion he proclaims the goodness and grandeur of the Stuarts, while he denounces with a gasping ferocity the infamous machinations of all covenants and presbyteries. With greater fulness than ever he describes his baffled ambitions. "I would have been," he writes, "a Mæcenas to the scholar, a pattern to the soldier, a favorer of the merchant, a protector of the tradesman and upholder of the yeoman, had not the impetuosity of the usurer overthrown my resolutions, and blasted my aims in the bud."

But above all he deplores his poverty for the sake of Cromarty. The disappointment of the hope he cherished for his native town was more poignantly grievous than the failure of the Universal Language or the loss of his manuscripts after Worcester fight. If only Sir Thomas had entered upon an unencumbered inheritance, the history of the world's commerce would have been changed. The ships of all nations might have sailed between the protecting Suters into that harbour, where in the wildest hurricane a fleet of ten thousand might find safe anchorage. Many a merchant adventurer had promised to send his richest argosies to Cromarty, and nothing could have impeded the success of the project save the baseness of Inverness. Was not Sir Philbert Vernati, who had "a great ascendant in counsel over all the adventurous merchants of what nation soever," resolved to make the fortune of Cromarty and its sheriff? On every side mines would have been open; the pick would have been heard in a hundred quarries. Italy would have sent northwards her best skilled artificers, while "men of literature and exquisite spirits of invention" would have taught Cromarty to surpass Aberdeen herself in poetry and learning. But, alas! Sir Thomas Urquhart was not allowed to aggrandise his estate. His enemies still lay in wait, "cannibal-like to swallow him up at a breakfast." Inverness looks with disdain upon her hapless rival, and Cromarty remains to-day the highland village of the seventeenth century.

Such is the sum of Sir Thomas Urquhart's original achievement, and the style in which his treatises are composed falls not an inch below his ingenious fancy. Like many another Scot, like Hawthornden, like Thomson, like Robert Louis Stevenson, he wrote English as a foreign tongue, which he had acquired after painful effort. You cannot read a page without being convinced that English was to him not the language of common speech, but a strange instrument, which at the touch of a master should yield a lofty sounding music. The style which he conquered was as remote from his native Scots as Greek or Latin, and he decorated it with a curious elaboration, which proves that he recognised the difference between literature and conversation. There is, perhaps, a touch of pedantry in his scrupulous avoidance of Scottish words. A diligent search has revealed but one, and the avoidance is the more remarkable because he had no aversion to the slang and proverbs of the street. But the *flytings*, those masterpieces of Amœbean scurrility, which doubtless he knew well and which encouraged his habit of stringing synonyms, exerted no more than a general influence upon him, and this influence is more noticeable in his *Rabelais* than in his original treatises.

His vocabulary is vast and various; he pilfered a dozen languages and all the sciences that he might enlarge it; nor does he ever hesitate to invent such words as are lacking to his purpose. He frankly avows his detestation of what is common or obvious. Where others would employ a paraphrase, he is quick to invent so new a term as *scripturiency* or *nixurience*. "Preface" being without significance, he prefers (after Mathurin Régnier) "epistle liminary"; and in the use of such strange compounds as *accresce* he is as ingenious as the decadents of ten years ago. Moreover, he defends his practice in a passage which will serve as a plea for a free vocabulary: "that which makes this disease (the paucity of words) the more incurable is that, when an exuberant spirit would to any high researched conceit adapt a peculiar word of his own coining, he is branded with incivility, if he apologise not for his boldness with a *quod ita dixerim, parcant Ciceronianæ manes, ignoscat Demosthenis genius*, and other such phrases, acknowledging his fault of making use of words never uttered by others, or at least by such as were most renowned for eloquence." And he assuredly asks no pardon from the shade of Cicero, but straightway declares that the Indians "were very temulencious symposiasts," while presently he proceeds to denounce the mean as "cluster-fists," and to reproach the Presbyterians with their "blinkard minds."

His style, again, was curiously shaped by his study of science, and mathematical metaphors are found on every page. Thus he describes the effect of Crichton's apparition: "The affections of the beholders, like so many several diameters drawn from the circumference of their various intents, did all encounter in the point of his perfection." On the other hand no artifice is too familiar, if his mood be flippant. "How now, pescods on it!" he cries when he has forgotten a name; or he will confuse a piece of new-fangled science with the slang of the minute. And you can forgive a writer a dozen faults who calls his enemy a "pristinary lobcock." Moreover, he has a constant care for the rhythm of his prose; he wrote with his ear as well as with his brain, and knew well how to set his periods to music. Where the poor apostle of simplicity at any price would write "backgate," Sir Thomas prefers "some secret angiport and dark postern door;" and the advantage both for sound and expression is on the side of Sir Thomas. From so vast a volume of eloquence it is difficult to select, but this reproof of the Presbyterians for their treatment of kings displays the more modest qualities of Urquhart's prose: "For of a king they only make use for their own ends, and so they will of any other supreme magistracy that is not of their own erection. Their kings are but as the kings of Lacedæmon, whom the Ephors presumed to fine for any small offence; or as the puppy kings which after children have trimmed with bits of taffeta, and ends of silver lace, and set upon wainscoat cupboards beside marmalade and sugar-cakes, are oftentimes disposed of, even by those that did pretend so much respect unto them for a two-penny custard, a pound of figs, or a mess of cream."

But he is not always thus restrained; he is apt to forget proportion, or, in his own simile, to put such a "porch upon a cottage as better befits a cathedral." Yet he would be punctilious in his adaptation of words to thoughts. The conclusion of the *Exquisite Jewel*, the most complicated rhapsody in English prose, is nothing else than an apology for its simple reticence. "I could," he confesses, "have enlarged this discourse with a choicer variety of phrase, and made it overflow the field of the reader's understanding, with an inundation of greater eloquence. . . . I could have introduced, in case of obscurity, synonymal, exargastick, and palilogetick elucidations; for sweetness of phrase, antimetathetick commutations of epithets." But he quenched his ardour; he "adhibited to the embellishment of his tractate" none of these tropes or figures, because for the moment "the matter was more prevalent with him than the superficial formality of a quaint discourse." In such wise does he formulate his theory of the relation of sound to sense, and if you did not recognise the sincerity of his humour, you might believe that for once he was laughing at his reader's innocence.

Never once in all his works does he mention Rabelais, though in his astounding genealogy as in his extravagant diction he pays him the compliment of imitation. Yet it is to his translation of Gargantua and Pantagruel that Urquhart owes his immortality, and surely no man better deserves the wreath of undying fame. His masterpiece shares the honour with our own Authorised Version of being the finest translation ever made from one language into another. The English lacks none of the abounding life and gaiety which make the original a perpetual joy. In fact it is not a translation at all: had Rabelais been a Briton, it is precisely in these terms that he would have written his golden book. It might have been composed afresh, as was the original "in eating and drinking." The very spirit of Rabelais breathes again in this perfect version, which, without the dimmest appearance of effort, echoes the very rhythm of the French, and for all its ingenuity of phrase and proverb, resolutely respects the duty of interpretation. But failure was impossible from the beginning: once in the history of the world a master of language found the task for which his genius was eminently adapted.

In point of style, Urquhart was Rabelais reincarnate. If Master Alcofribas handled a vocabulary of surpassing richness, Sir Thomas, the most travelled man of his age, had stored his memory with the pearls of five languages. Science and slang were the hobbies of each, and both Scot and Frenchman were as quick to find his metaphors in the gutter as to gather them after thoughtful research in the solemn treatises of the middle age. But above all, it is in his treatment of slang that Urquhart shows his supremacy. His courage is as great as his knowledge, and bookish as he was, he kept his ears always alert to the quick impressions of the street. The Puritan, who, finding not enough immorality in life to glut his censure, invests simple words with vice, has wreaked his idle fury on the dead Sir Thomas, and more than once has dragged his masterpiece into the malefactor's dock. But the masterpiece remains to defy the Puritan, as it defies the critic, and it is no less assured of eternity than its magnificent original. To belaud its perfection is to confess its blemishes, yet its blemishes lean ever to the side of excellence. Though Urquhart crept into the very skin of Rabelais, at times the skin sits a little tightly upon him. He outdoes Rabelais even in extravagance, thereby achieving what might have seemed a plain impossibility. When the master exhausts every corner of human knowledge or human life in a list of synonyms, Urquhart is always ready to increase the list from the limitless depths of his own research. One list of thirteen he has expanded to thirty-six ; another famous chapter he has doubled in length ; and yet every line bears the true impress of Rabelais. Again, at times he is apt to explain rather than to interpret ; but his explanation is so rigidly within the boundaries of the original, that not even the pedant can find heart to protest. As for his mistakes, they are condoned by their magnificence; and if now and then he says what Rabelais did not, you wonder which has the better of it, the original or the version.

Like all great works, Urquhart's translation had its forerunner; and its forerunner was Randle Cotgrave, without whose superb dictionary * the *Rabelais* might never have been accomplished. It is the common superstition of the schools that the use of a dictionary is fatal to the acquisition of a full and free vocabulary. Yet here is Urquhart, whose eccentric vocabulary has never been surpassed, working with a dictionary at his elbow. Now, Cotgrave's "bundle of words," as his modesty styles it, contains such fagots as never before were collected by mortal man. No wonder his French colleague declares that he had read books of every kind and in every dialect, nor is it strange that, writing at the very beginning of the seventeenth century, he should have made a generous use of Rabelais. But he was one of those to whom words are living, breathing things, with colour and character of their own, and his dictionary, which Shakespeare may have used, can still be read with the rapidity and excitement of a romance. In his love of synonyms, he rivalled Urquhart; like Urquhart, he would never content himself with one word when twenty were available. A famous naturalist, he helped

* A Dictionarie of the French and English Tongues. Compiled by Randle Cotgrave. London: Printed by Adam Islip. Anno 1611.

the translator at the point wherein his weakness was most palpably confessed, and the names of strange birds and beasts may easily be traced to their authentic source.

Cotgrave, moreover, packs into his book—this "verball creature," and indeed it is "a creature," a living thing—all the folklore and superstition of his age; and here again he was a sure guide to the footsteps of Urquhart. But Urquhart followed him even in his errors. To quote an example: "friar John of the Funnels" is at least as celebrated as "frère Jean des Entommeures," and you wonder where Urquhart found his false translation, until you consult the page of Cotgrave, which refers you from *Entommeure* to *Entonnoir*, which being interpreted is a *funnel*. And thus it is that in English friar John takes the title, which he will never lose, not from the "cuttings" or "carvings," but from the Funnels. Of Cotgrave himself we know nothing, save that he dedicated his dictionary to "the Right Honourable, and my very good Lord and Maister, Sir William Cecil, *Knight*, *Lord* Burghley, *and sonne* and heire apparant unto the Earle of Exceter." But never in any enterprise were three masters so admirably matched as these three: Rabelais, Cotgrave, Urquhart. And who shall say which of the three within his limits was the greatest?

Urquhart translated Rabelais, and had they been of the same century Rabelais would have flouted the hero, who gave him a second life. For as in style

Urquhart was the last of the Elizabethans, so in science he resumed the fallacies of the Middle Ages. He regarded with a childish reverence the many problems, at which Rabelais laughed from the comfortable depth of his easy chair. And there is a delightful irony in the truth, that this perfect translator was in his own original essays nothing else than Rabelais stripped of humour. He would discuss the interminable stupidities of the schoolmen with a grave face and ceaseless ingenuity. He had no interest in aught save the unattainable. To square the circle and perfect the Universal Language were the least of his enterprises. And here we touch the tragedy of his life. He was like the man he met at Venice, "who believed he was sovereign of the whole Adriatic Sea, and sole owner of all the ships that came from the Levant." His madness—for it was nothing less—inspired him with the confidence that all things were possible to his genius. He was Don Quixote with a yet wilder courage. "I do promise," he says somewhere, "shortly to display before the world ware of greater value than ever from the East Indies was brought in ships to Europe"; and straightway he pictures himself another Andromeda, chained to the rock of hard usage, and exposed to the merciless dragon usury, beseeching "the sovereign authority of the country, like another Perseus mounted on the winged Pegasus of respect to the weal and honour thereof, to relieve us, by their power, from the eminent danger of the jaws of so wild a monster."

But, despite his madness, he was in many aspects wise beyond the wisdom of his generation. When all the world was resolute in the persecution of witches, he looked upon witchcraft with a sensible scepticism worthy of Reginald Scot. He would leave all men free to speculate in theology ; for, says he, every one, if he be sincere, will confess that he has his own religion. Even in his discourse upon the Universal Language there is many a generalisation, which, when set forth many years after by Lord Monboddo and others, was deemed a marvel of intelligence. In politics, above all, he was inspired to a noble patriotism. He insisted with all his eloquence upon the union of England and Scotland. He would have compelled the general use of Great Britain for a title, and he pleaded that Scots should find the same equal privileges in London, which had long since been granted them by the city of Paris. Withal his character was gay, sanguine, and honourable, as George Glover, who drew him from the life, has worthily suggested. The portrait, indeed, is rarely characteristic of Urquhart's elegance and foppery. The pose declares the happy assurance of a hero, half-duellist, half-orator, as quick to use his tongue as his sword, while the huge rosettes, emphasised by a slim figure, are at once the symbol and the measure of the Cavalier's vanity. But for all his vanity he was so honest a gentleman, that he would never change an opinion for the sake of profit, and persisted in his just condemnation of the Kirk and Parliament, even when he was suing his enemies for their consideration. Of his amiability and courage there is no doubt. With characteristic candour he declares that he has never coveted the goods of any man; he has never violated the trust reposed in him; he has given ground to no enemy before the day of Worcester. That he is surnamed Parresiastes, or Free of Speech, is his favourite boast; for he loves ever to be open-hearted and of an explicit discourse. What wonder is it, then, that in the triumph of traitors and covenants, he should have been easily discomfited?

He left no school, and only one imitator: the Earl of Worcester, hapless and ingenious as himself. This nobleman echoed the career of Urquhart perforce, and echoed of set purpose his language and research. He, too, met ruin on Worcester field; he, too, spent his eloquence in the hopeless demand for liberty, a favour which he too would have repaid by discoveries no less marvellous than the new language. Freedom for him meant the discovery of the steam-engine and a revolution in the art of war; and he pleaded for freedom in the very terms used by Urquhart. He, too, had lost his notes, and the title of the treatise * which he was not permitted to publish, and which he also valued at many thousands of pounds, might have been composed by the author of the *Exquisite Jewel.*

* Thus it runs: "A century of the Names and Scantlings of such Inventions, as at present I can call to mind to have tried and perfected (my former notes being lost)"—with much more to the same purpose.

Thus a single generation produced these two men, whose eccentric genius and unmerited misfortune give them a place apart in the history of the world. Urquhart's misery is the more acute, for the greater height of his aspirations. His life was marred by broken ambitions, and made by one surpassing masterpiece. His manifold schemes of progress and of scholarship died with the brain which they inhabited. The Italian artificers and French professors whom he bade to Cromarty never obeyed the invitation; the castle which once stood upon the South Suter was so fiercely demolished, that the place of its foundation is left unmarked. The vulgar reputation of Hugh Miller has persuaded the town, whereof Sir Thomas was sheriff, to forget that it was the birthplace of a great man. But the translation of Rabelais remains, and that will only die with the death of Pantagruel himself.